Turin

Approaching Animals

David Brooks

Also by David Brooks

Novels
The House of Balthus
The Fern Tattoo
The Umbrella Club
The Conversation

Short Fiction
The Book of Sei and Other Stories
Sheep and the Diva
Black Sea
Napoleon's Roads

Poetry
The Cold Front
Walking to Point Clear
Urban Elegies
The Balcony
Open House

Non-fiction
The Necessary Jungle: Literature and Excess
De/scription: A Balthus notebook
*The Sons of Clovis: Ern Malley, Adoré Floupette, and
a Secret History of Australian Poetry*
Derrida's Breakfast
The Grass Library
Animal Dreams

Turin

Approaching Animals

David Brooks

Brandl & Schlesinger

First published by Brandl & Schlesinger in 2021
PO Box 127 Blackheath NSW 2785 Australia
www.brandl.com.au

ISBN 978-0-6452350-1-2 (print)
ISBN 978-0-6452350-2-9 (epdf)
ISBN 978-0-6452350-3-6 (epub)

A catalogue record for this book is available from
the National Library of Australia

Cover and book design by Andras Berkes-Brandl

To the angels of Animal Liberation

ACKNOWLEDGEMENTS

For help and encouragement at various points in the development of this work, I'd like to thank Helen Bergen, Andras Berkes-Brandl, Igor Brbre, Andrew Burke, Jason Grossman, Jeffrey and Leila Masson, Ray Mjadwesch, Mateja Prešern, Scott Stephens, Veronica Sumegi, Špela Šuškovič, Christine Townend and Stuart White, and to thank the University of Sydney for facilities afforded me as an Honorary Associate Professor in the School of Letters, Art and Media in its Faculty of Social Sciences. Above all – our ovid companions Henry, Jonathan, Jason, and Orpheus Pumpkin notwithstanding – I'd like to express my deep gratitude to Teja Brooks Pribac, without whose conversation, support and inspiration this book, like so much else, would have been quite literally impossible.

Four of these pieces ('Where Does it Stop', 'Regard', 'Face' and 'Dark Places'), collated by Scott Stephens, were published as 'A Critique of Pure Reason' on the Australian Broadcasting Corporation's Religion and Ethics page on 8 April 2019.

CONTENTS

1
Turin

In Turin, on the 3rd of January 1889, Friedrich Nietzsche experienced a breakdown from which he was never fully to recover. He'd been staying in a house overlooking the Piazza Carlo Alberto. Apparently, on that day, he'd seen a man cruelly flogging a horse at the other end of the piazza and had run to the animal, thrown his arms around its neck to protect it, said something to it, doubtless to comfort it (I'm uncomfortable with the 'it': was the horse a mare, a stallion, a gelding?) and had then fallen to the ground, slipping into a coma that lasted two days and from which he returned so impaired he is said to have quite lost his mind, hardly ever to have spoken again.

The story is disputed. Perhaps it says more about the prejudice of people at the time – and for most of the time since – that trying to save a horse from a flogging would be associated with the onset of madness. I can't see any reason not to think of it as the onset of a kind of deep sanity.

Ironically, you could say that Nietzsche's career began and ended with a horse. In 1868, at the age of twenty-four, while serving a year in a Prussian artillery division in Naumburg, he'd struck his chest on the pommel of a saddle while mounting – he was apparently a fine horseman – and tore some muscles in his side so badly he was debilitated for months. Unable to continue with the artillery division, he turned to the completion of his studies in philology. But that, while monumental in its way, is of no great matter here. What matters – if anyone heard the words, no one recorded them – is what Nietzsche *said* to the horse. Or perhaps just the act of saying itself: the saying and, afterward, the silence.

2
Language Creatures

We have fashioned the difference between non-human animals and ourselves as one of language, and I will accede to that. Nietzsche himself, as it happens (not that this is to be a book about Nietzsche), has a direct and concise offering on the subject:

> The significance of language for the evolution of culture lies in this, that mankind set up in language a separate world beside the other world, a place it took to be so firmly set that, standing upon it, it could lift the rest of the world off its hinges and make itself master of it. To the extent that man has for long ages believed in the concepts and names of things as in *aeternae veritates* he has appropriated to himself that pride by which he raised himself above the animal; he really thought that in language he possessed knowledge of the world.
>
> —*Human, All Too Human* (1878)[1]

But when we speak of language in this manner we speak within severe restraints, essentially those of a power-arrangement, like those described several decades ago by Edward Said in his *Orientalism* (1978). One preserves one's power (a) by not allowing those over whom one would maintain that power to have anything but the most limited and utilitarian access to one's own language, so that one can think of them as savage, illiterate, etc., and (b) by not condescending to learn, let alone use, *their* language. Language and its withholding, in other words, are implements of power. We say that 'animals', by which we mean non-*human* animals – but let us name a few specifically: dogs, cats, pigs, sheep, kangaroos, rats, … the list is as long as one's patience – do not have 'language', when what we mean is that they do not have *our* language, and that we will not condescend to even identify, let alone learn, theirs.

We do not know what our relationships would be if these matters were otherwise: if we defined language differently, say, or if we *opened*, as in set aside our assumptions of or demands for power.

These things are not complex, but neither are they very likely to be done. Perhaps all we can ask or hope for – and we must at least ask – is that it be acknowledged that what we have for so long held to be a truth of our relationship and the definition of our distinction, is to this extent a matter of power, and preservation of power, in effect an intellectual violence, to ourselves perhaps no less than to non-human animals. *We* define what 'language' is, *we* define what a 'word' is, *we* define what a 'syntactical construction' is, what an 'act of communication' is, in part by refusing to consider as such languages and acts of communication that we are unwilling and unwitting witnesses to every day. What of the languages of breath, of gesture, of eyes, of smell; what of voices so high, so low, so compressed or so rapid, that we can hardly register them as voices at all?

3

Mind. Being. World.

Mind. Being. World. Inadequate as these notions are they are pretty much all we have in terms of representing our conceptualisations of whatever it is we find ourselves living through every day, whether these days be those of the wild adventurer or the local council worker. They, or the things that they attempt to capture and explain, are our familiars, the lenses by which we see or attempt to see everything we encounter, feel and experience.

They have been presented, of course, as tools for the understanding of *human* being, *human* world, *human* mind, but it's inconceivable that non-human animals don't have them too. Very likely for each species each one of these things will be different. A dog can hear and smell far beyond the human range and in this sense – in these dimensions – his/her immediate World may be larger than a human's. We could say that each species looks out upon that Greater World, in which what humans may wish to call World is a kind of bubble of consciousness, through a different window, from a different angle. Angles may be different, some windows may be large, others small, but one senses that dimension has little to do with it, is either irrelevant or naïve. The point is that we are all in it together, every species, *all* species; we – dog, sheep, duck, cicada, human, ant – partake in Being, we partake in Mind, we partake in World.

Martin Heidegger – for of all contemporary or near-contemporary philosophers it is perhaps he who has most influentially (and controversially) attempted to sort out these things – says that animals are 'poor in world' (*Being and Time*, 1927), and, by implication, that humans are rich in it. We could expect no other position with regard to a concept that humans have devised essentially for their own use, to facilitate their own survival in and manipulation *of* that World. But even in this derogation of the (non-human) 'animal' world Heidegger is admitting that 'animals' have it too, that 'world' applies to them as much as to humans. And, ironically, if we can admit as we have learned to do – as I don't think Heidegger ever could – that humans themselves are animals, then he can be seen to be pointing (not very consciously) to the limitations of our 'World' also.

The point is important for all sorts of reasons, but let's just say for now that it is important 'for our respect for the other beings around us'. This sense that they too have a *weight* and *intensity* of being, of experience. That it is not a matter of size. That a duck or a rat or a cicada can have his or her glory days, his or her days of toil, his or her days of devastating tragedy (T., cleaning up sheep poop at the top of the paddock yesterday near the duck-pond, looked across and there was a female wood duck – she thinks the mother of the brood of four ducklings who first appeared four days ago, but who seem all to have died or been killed since – standing alone by the pond, and she said – but who can know these things? – that she seemed to be disoriented, demented somehow, to have *lost her mind*), and that as we open ourselves to this aspect of the being of others – that if we look at them *as if we shared* such things – we can find our own being, mind, world, our own *portions* of Being,

Mind and World, incrementally (if only infinitesimally) expanding. The realm is unknown to us, we do not *know* what we receive; we may not even have words for it, since the words we do have are for things that we've already experienced. But there will be arcings, moments of strange accession. In the past we might have called them mystic. But that is to hold such moments at bay. It is not inconceivable that they one day become our familiars.

The point is important in that way, yes, but that's not why I make it. Human animals have come to dominate the world. In innumerable ways. I cannot conceive of a non-human animal that has not been influenced by the existence of human animals. Pollution, climate change, destruction of habitat have reached even those parts of the planet (such as they are) that humans have not yet physically reached. And for a huge number of non-human animals the impact has been profound, devastating. Human impact is responsible for most of the extinctions in human memory, but as it happens I'm referring to species still *in* existence. If Heidegger, in saying that 'animals are poor in world', is right in any sense, then it is perhaps in this one, that we have impacted upon, damaged, and deprived them of much of their World, in effect *stolen it from them*.

Most sheep, for example, go to slaughter at little over twelve months of age, when in 'human' terms they are barely more than four years old – barely, that is, out of infancy. How much World do we deprive a creature of, when we deprive him/her of fourteen fifteenths of his/her possible lifespan? And if, as I know all too well, a sheep can be rescued from this horrid mill, it will still be for a life of constraint, manipulation, confinement, if only to 'protect' him/her, 'for [his/her] own good'. In this sense I think it is very true to say that 'animals' in the world as we now have it, non-human animals, live *within the human*, just as, say – though I think in more insidious and pervasive ways – the people of lands conquered by the Romans (or the British, the Belgians, the Dutch, the…) lived inside *those* worlds. And although this may seem paradoxical they are also to some degree therefore *within us*. The 'animal' has long –

perennially, perpetually – been regarded as the 'Outside' of philosophy. This is one of the main reasons Philosophy has always failed non-human animals so badly. We think of the Animal as *outside*, but No; we – humans – have affected, influenced everything: the Animal is *inside*, a wildcard in our guts (our Mind, our Being, our World).

4

Twilight

At the time of his breakdown, Nietzsche was seeing through the press a work called *The Twilight of the Idols*. Twilight, a time between things, literally a between-light. I had always presumed that that was in fact its etymology, that *twi* meant *between*, but in fact it means *two*. All the better. W.B. Yeats thought – or recorded the Celtic thought – that twilight was a dangerous but also magical time, when one could escape the human world, or be abducted from it by the Sidhe (pron. *Shee*), the marauding tribes of Faery, who ride out, in that *crack between worlds*, and pluck humans away. But even for Yeats it was broader than that. His most famous expression of it is from a tale, in *Stories of Red Hanrahan* (1897), called 'The Twisting of the Rope':

> day by day as he wandered slowly and aimlessly he passed deeper and deeper into that great Celtic twilight, in which heaven and earth so mingle that each seems to have taken upon itself some shadow of the other's beauty

I like the thought that this passage had been recycled from an earlier piece, published in 1892, in which the last word was not 'beauty' but 'tragedy', as if even the passage itself were written in two lights.

Twilight is the time when the earth is lit not by the sun directly but by the sun's reflection in the atmosphere in the period just before dawn and just after sunset. An un-earthly time in one sense, but also a very earthly one in another, or at least a time when, because one cannot see as clearly as one could see before (or will afterward), the earth seems charged with mystery. A time when one's mind finds itself between two different modes or realms of thought; when one realm has not quite become, or transitioned to, the other; a time of ambivalences, ambiguities, antinomies, doubts, uncertainties, paradoxes – things being, and being seen, *this* way but also *that*. There are even, as I have just found in the *Oxford English Dictionary*, *twi-thoughts*, which is to say *vague* or *indistinct* thoughts. One can be said to be *twi-minded*. As if thought itself trembled or, to continue the light imagery, *shimmered*.

5
Where Does It Stop?

Where does it stop? That tiresome question with which, it can sometimes seem, all 'animal' people and vegans are relentlessly assailed. Where does *refuge* stop? Where does your compassion reach its limit? Where will your refusal to kill/eat stop? And all of the corollaries, most commonly – pronounced as if it were some kind of trump card – the assertion that 'every thing you eat *lives*, every thing you eat *feels*; surely, if you're consistent, you'll end up eating only air, and even that is full of living things!'

I am advised not to confront this question directly – not to *go into this place* – but (with the proviso that veganism is a *work in progress*, and that there is no reason why – the suffering of animals being so urgent a matter – it should suspend or restrain itself while it searches for answers) the mind, trained as it is to think 'logically', goes back to it, over and again, banging itself against this wall, looking for an exit, a solution, an adequate response.

Setting aside one's suspicion that their real question is *where, amongst the animate creatures of this world, can we start eating again?* as if the killing and eating of animate creatures were somehow fundamental to their being (most vegans I know have simply decided to avoid eating *any* animate creatures, whether or not they are 'sentient', or can suffer in any way fellow humans might recognise as such), what is the logic of the questioners here?

That if one cannot avoid *all* suffering, then it is somehow *unreasonable* to avoid *any*? That if one can't save all then why save any at all? That if there is some creature you might inadvertently harm, then you relinquish your right to care for others?

Despite the fact that their questioning is itself almost always flying in the face of reason – no amount of logical reasoning will persuade most people to change their dietary habits in this regard, and yet it's very often these same people who insist upon logical, reasoned responses – one is convinced that there is, *has* to be, an answer, even if it's only some understanding of why it is that such a question cannot *be* readily answered.

Where *does* it stop?

The concern, when this question is asked, is rarely for the vegan/'animalist' involved, or for any other living being, let alone for receiving or considering an answer, but instead to reach, like a sad and familiar punch-line, that point when, by supposedly exposing a radical inconsistency in veganism and in so doing reducing it to an absurdity, a *non sequitur*, the asker can absolve him-

or herself of any further conscience in the matter and, by a further abuse of logic, feel affirmed in his or her Carnism.[2]

Numerous attempts have nevertheless been made to provide answers to this question – *the* Question – and most have failed. Most recently, in the long and ancient history of such attempts (for surely they were asked even of Pythagoras), there has been the argument of *sentience*, most famously articulated by Peter Singer, whereby it is *sentient* creatures – creatures who various tests and observations have seemed to demonstrate have the *ability to feel*, and so possess a major prerequisite of what we call *consciousness* – that one does not eat, presumably because beyond that level, that cut-off point, the creatures one eats cannot feel that that is what's happening to them, are unable to experience what we understand as suffering.

In *Animal Liberation* (1975) Singer situated that cut-off point, that barrier, at the *oyster*. I am not about to take on the issue of where this barrier should be drawn. (Somehow, confoundingly, this argument-by-sentience has become intertwined with a point about *movement*; the oyster is a bivalve mollusc, but, although it does have a *foot*, unlike other such molluscs does not, in its 'adulthood', have the ability to *go* anywhere.) Nor, at the risk of seeming to cede ground immediately to those I attempt to answer, will I pretend that the question of sentience isn't a deeply problematic one.

The question of sentience, of comparability (of brain size and function, of the capacity to experience emotions that *we* recognize), while I can see and must admit that we cannot do without it, only shows how far we've gone wrong. Why then does it exist? What further (larger?) question does it enable us to deal with or keep at bay? Is it that we must have a cut-off point, for fear that if our compassion extends too far we will starve? Or that the quality of our lives will be intolerably diminished? Or is it a matter of our self-*image*, the assumption that creatures must be *of our club* before they become entitled to our compassion?

The very scientists and sceptics who argue against anthropomorphism are the ones we most often find demanding proof of similarity. A further *non sequitur*: the question is not a/the question, but an 'intellectualising' of a fundamental will-not-to-change. We argue, but – leaving aside, when we assert that these creatures are to be respected the *more* they are like us, that it is *we* who are the problem (what does it *mean* to say 'like *us*'?) – argument was never the point.

Do I fail to answer the question? Probably. But such failure may not be quite what it appears to be. The supposed dominion over non-human animals is at the core of our logos. It would be erroneous, I think, to imagine that that mode of thought which led us *into* so cruel an assumption and has sustained us within it for so long is going to be able to lead us very easily and convincingly *out* of it. To the question implicit in all of the questions above – *When will we/you see reason?* – one might respond: When will you see that there is *more than* reason (or, perhaps, that there are more *kinds* of reason than *that* one)?

It is not *reason* that leads most 'animal' people to their position of resistance to the prevailing cruelty of the societies in which they find themselves, not *reason* which brings vegans – *ethical* vegans (for there are different kinds) – to their positions of refusal. At least, not reason alone. Although it's not unusual for them to come to feel that their position is almost quintessentially one of reason, and that this reason, when presented to others, must surely prevail, reason alone is rarely sufficient to change the course of those whom they find themselves trying to convince. Something else is required.

It is not that reason will not work to bring about a change (of habit, of diet, of attitude), but without this 'something else' this change is unlikely to be sustained. It is common to refer to this other thing as a *change of heart*. Others refer to it as a matter of *revelation* – of, say, *having one's eyes peeled*. All of these expressions are awkward, as we might expect of the submerged or discounted terms of a binary, the other, dominant part of which is attached, oyster-like, to the prevailing *Logos*.

6

Regard

Regard. What we choose to look at, or find ourselves looking at. It's often in moments of something like *absentmindedness*, when conscious thought is in a measure suspended, that we find ourselves looking at, and able to see, the smaller creatures (and, I admit, it's most often *movement* that has attracted our attention). That bridge – also often crossed in the absence of conscious thought – between observation and empathy, or, if it does not go that far, at least recognition of something in the creature's activity, a sense in which we seem to *know* what he/she is doing, even if he/she is 'only' a beetle rolling a ball of dung (we see that he/she is struggling, see that he/she is managing, *how* he/she is managing). There is an extension of ourselves in such moments that is a beginning, an opening.

I watch my dog sleeping. Sit there, quietly, attending. See him breathing. Feel myself breathing. See him adjusting the position of his forepaw or his hind leg as he sleeps, or rises from sleep enough to do so. I know why I adjust my own sleeping posture. Because my shoulder aches, say, or my hand has gone numb, or one nostril has become blocked and I'll perhaps breathe more easily if I lie on my other side. Reasons that might also explain *his* changes of posture. Sometimes, for me, it's just restlessness. Just as sometimes *he* must be restless. What makes *him* restless? What makes *me* restless? Too much *thought*? We share these things, this physicality, *that is more than physicality*: the mind *in* the body, the body-mind. He sighs. What about? Can we say that a dog cannot sigh for the same kind of reason that a human sighs?

I don't know what it is to be a dog, but I know what it is to breathe, to feel the breath entering and leaving; I know what it is to seek the most comfortable position in which to sleep; I know how a sigh will sometimes escape me, as some thought or another passes, a regret, a sorrow. We are worlds apart, it may be, but we are also a world together.

7

Face

We don't have to *prove* animals to humans, or (as I should say, at every point in this book) *non-human* animals to human animals. That huge mistake dominates our human-animal discourse. The mind of *human* animals – and the immense damage it has done, the labyrinths that it cannot find its way out of – is a *human* problem. Always this special pleading. Through behaviourism, through neuro-science, through (even) the Cambridge Declaration on Consciousness, marvellous as I think their findings and arguments have often been. Non-human animals, we have felt too long, must be shown to have attributes and characteristics that we share or at the very least *recognise*, that accord with *our* understandings of being.

In all our dealings with and about non-human animals, this is to say, we cannot eliminate our own face. To say nothing of its corollary: that they must recognise *us*. So often, in my observation of the interaction of human animals with non-human animals, this need, in the former, to be allowed to touch, this need to be *seen*, this need to be *responded* to in some way that can be seen as positive and/or accepting – this need to be *thanked*, this *in*ability to co-exist (let alone assist, protect) *without condition*.

8

Protocol

A friend – a champion of the rights of animals – finds the mere presence of a non-human animal – he speaks of cows – to be soothing, meditative, an almost spiritual event, and wishes more human animals would seek out such experiences, to increase their sensitivity toward and understanding of non-human ones. Another friend, who has established and manages a sanctuary for rescued farm animals, is happy to have people visit and meet those animals, and interact with them – indeed has just established, as so many such sanctuaries do, the practice of a periodic open day as a fund-raising event and a means of educating the public about the plight of animals in this age of industrial farming. With regard to the former it could be objected that, however placid as she may appear, the cow in such a situation does not have a great deal of choice in the matter, and may not, herself, be enjoying the experience at all. With regard to the latter it could be argued that to display non-human animals in such a manner – to make them available to the human gaze and touch – is actually a violation of the sanctuary one has offered them; that a sanctuary should seek to be as much as possible a freedom from *all* forms of instrumentalisation, even those which can be framed as furthering the interests of the sanctuary itself. Are these positions irreconcilable? What are the protocols of sanctuary?

We, my partner and I, are hardly innocent. We have visited sanctuaries ourselves, and taken joy in our encounters with animals there. But to go in amongst them? To *reach* for them? To seek to *touch* them, even if that touch is merely to stroke, or no more than a laying-on of the hand? Seeking to touch a stranger in a bus or park or street or lecture-hall would not often be welcomed and might well lead to a charge of assault. Why should we think differently of non-human animals? That someone has given them sanctuary – that *we* have given it them – does not give us the right to touch them at will, even if we might want to do so out of the purest of affection, and certainly it does not obligate *them*; otherwise, surely, it would not *be* sanctuary.

It will be objected that there are non-human animals who *like* to be handled, *like* to be touched. Very well, and when we can be sure of this we can perhaps make exceptions, but let's not presume, automatically, an animal's compliance, let alone pleasure; indeed let's go further and envision situations in which the choice and mode of engagement are as much the (non-human) animal's as they are the human's.

9

The Gaze

Why, to our thought, to our *thinking* our thought, is the Gaze so important? Firstly, of course – it must be admitted – because some person or persons have theorised it. John Berger, Maurice Blanchot, Jacques Lacan, Luce Irigaray, etc. – quite a few people, probably hundreds. And the trope at the theory's heart – that the eye (and so the gaze), inseparable from the operation of our Logos, is central not only to our attempts to know and dominate the world about us, but to our individuation within that world – has become established.

One key document in the evolution of this theory is Lacan's 'The Mirror Stage as formative of the function of the *I*' (1949). Another is Blanchot's 'The Gaze of Orpheus' (1955). The gaze of Orpheus – we need no reminding – sends Eurydice back to Hell. But of course it was not, originally, a gaze, merely a look: something in our modern condition has turned it, via our theory, into *gaze*.[3]

Is that – the sending them back to Hell – what our gaze does when we turn it upon non-human animals, or is this just another instance of a myth getting in the way, underpinning our isolation, helping to keep us enclosed within our human bubble? (The myth, it may be, tells us *not* to look.)

What *is* it we refer to when we speak of *gaze*? Do we mean all and any periods of extended visual attention, or something more specific? A gaze is a lengthy focus of the eye upon an object. But so is the *stare* (and the aggression it can carry, the offence it often causes), and so are *surveillance*, *keeping an eye* on something, *watchfulness*. While we could argue that the gaze, per se, is more open, less motivated, has about it something of *contemplation* – i.e. if not of wonder, then of wondering about – I'm not sure how much it matters. Surely part of our understanding of the gaze (glance/look/stare) is that it's a complex thing, that it can perform more than one function. A buck kangaroo may stand high and stare at us. Is this in order to ensure that our focus is on him so that the rest of his mob can slip away? Is it, as I think we can be confident it is with most non-human animals who fix their eyes upon us, to track and appraise our movements, assess the danger we might represent? Is it to ward us off? Or is it because he finds us interesting, a creature he wants to look at? Surely there's a possibility it's all of these things.

Not all non-human animals depend upon the optic sense as much as the human animal does. The question as to whether there can be a *gaze of the ear*, let's say, or a *gaze of the nose* might lead us into some interesting territory. But I think we can say with some certainty that non-human animals watch us a great deal more than we watch them. It would be foolish, a species arrogance, to imagine that they don't think, don't wonder as they do so, and to fail to take the next step and ask ourselves, if we recognise, as clearly we must, that the non-human animal is a gazer in his/her own right, how we can say the things we say about the gaze of the *human* animal – that it is an attempt to 'know' and therefore dominate the world about us, that on the one hand it's inseparable from the operation/creation/sustenance of our Logos, and on the other is crucial in establishing a sense of self and individual identity – without extending those things to the *non-*human animal who gazes back?

And if we do, as I think logically we must, what then? What else might we then have to change about our thinking concerning that non-human animal's capacities, his/her sense of self, his/her intentions, etc.?

10
Triage

There is, always, so much work to be done in the areas of animal activism and advocacy. One can find oneself spread so thinly. In a recent interview, the first paramedic to arrive on the scene of a suicide bombing was asked how, with such grievous injury around her, she decided whom to treat first. She said she began with the first person she saw, no doubt – not that she added this – with her peripheral mind and vision trying to determine whom she'd help next.

What else can one do but treat the case immediately in front of one? I don't intend, in what follows, to propose a particular order or set of rules of triage, much as I suspect we're in need of one.

That's for others to do. I intend rather to attempt to identify one of the barriers they may encounter as they do so.

There are calls, from some animal rights theorists, for an avoidance of 'single issue' protest and advocacy. When one's ultimate aim is, as unquestionably it *should* be, the *abolition* of cruelty to and instrumentalisation of non-human animals, such thinking goes, then campaigning for *mitigations* of animal suffering – the prohibition of sow stalls, the banning of the mulesing of sheep, the insistence upon larger cages for battery hens, etc. (matters of *welfare* rather than *abolition*) – runs the great danger of creating an impression that, *if* these things are done, *if* these concessions are made, then the exploitation of these animals has become more acceptable and the greater issue somehow been dealt with, that a sort of compromise has been reached.

The problem can seem particularly stark when we apply a human filter. A great many of us agree the Australian government's policy of incarcerating, as if they were criminals, refugees and asylum seekers who have sought to come to Australia by boat – placing them, in effect, in concentration camps on islands far off-shore – has been a cruel and unacceptable one, as indeed it's been declared to be by the United Nations High Commission for Refugees.

The abolitionist criticism of welfarism, it could be argued, translated to this *human*-animal situation, is that it implies that, if conditions were improved for asylum-seeker prisoners in such remote detention centres – if they were given, say, tents of their own rather than having to share them, given greater exercise space, or better food, better entertainment systems, etc. – then their incarceration would be more acceptable, a proposition few, if any, of those who currently object to such incarceration would accept.

One suspects also, however, that few would want to see such ameliorations withheld from these incarcerated asylum seekers. Certainly I know few 'welfarists' who do not long for the abolition of industrial/factory farming, or at least for the day when it will be no more. Seeing that day as a long way off, however, and knowing that, meanwhile, billions of animals suffer horribly in factory farms and the like, they seek to improve, in the short term, the conditions in which these animals are forced to live.

The alternative – to refrain from seeking to improve those conditions, to leave those animals to suffer more than they might, and to press, instead, exclusively for the *abolition* of factory farming – is simply unacceptable to them, indeed, for most, impossible, given the compassion they feel. They cannot see that the one thing – helping animals in their present and urgent need – has to exclude the other. They can still protest vehemently the very existence of factory farming. They can still work in every way they can for its abolition. They would never concede that a negotiated amelioration of suffering would ever in any way make that suffering acceptable, or the causes of that suffering less heinous. And on the other hand I know few abolitionists who will not help an individual animal in need, or who would not welcome the news that animals in a factory farm are suffering less than they have been.

Clearly these positions are not incompatible. How have they come to be seen so? Whence the hard binary of Abolition vs Welfare? What is its driving factor? Is it a feeling that the energy and resources given to 'single issue' welfarist work will deplete the resources given to work upon the bigger issue? Is it a feeling that it is somehow not possible – that one does not have the persuasive and intellectual resources – to argue effectively for one while also engaging in the other? Are our emotional and intellectual resources so limited?

I don't dispute that Abolitionism makes an important point, or that Welfarists might learn from it the important lesson that they must try to ensure, in any amelioration of animal suffering they seek, that the message is not given out that factory farming might in any way become the more acceptable. Perhaps, in this regard, we might begin with the way we present the discussion in the first place, frame the ameliorations *as* abolitions – the *abolition* of sow stalls, the *abolition* of battery cages – rather than as *approvals* (of free range eggs, of stunning before slaughter). But, again, there aren't many who don't do this already, and I don't want to discount the real lessons that hard-line abolitionism might help us learn. (In addition to those already listed, for example, there's the danger that, in protesting for and negotiating single-issue ameliorations we might be falling victim to a regime of what Herbert Marcuse called Repressive Tolerance[4]; that the industries we fight against – the sources of the greatest animal suffering – *factor in*, systemically, the amelioration of the conditions that give rise to dissent in order to protect and extend their core activity.)

But as it happens I address the issue for a different reason, the manner in which this and other such dichotomies unnecessarily and counter-productively divide the growing community of those concerned with animal rights and animal advocacy.

Work for animals must be done, constantly, on many levels. Our best approach, in terms of animal suffering, must be multi-faceted. It's this work itself which is our axis. Welfarism and Abolitionism might, in some people's eyes, be the poles of that axis, but it's neither realistic nor helpful –

indeed may be harmfully divisive – to locate oneself at or confine oneself to either extremity.

And triage? As usual the secret may be to be looking about you. The first attention in most cases *is* to be paid to the suffering nearest one's fingertips. If one finds that this 'steals time' from other action, then there are options. Either one finds more time (let's say) or one waits, does what is most immediately in front of one in the thought that it contributes to the other, that each is a part of the other, and that the time for the other – the time for the time for the other – will certainly come.

11

The Shared Body

The animal me. The body I share, that I have in common with others. How I seem to hear, distantly, through it, their voices. How it *translates*. Though even that, there, is a betrayal, an abstraction. It's not *voices*. It's something deeper and other than that. And a humbling, before them – those other animals – that might never otherwise have happened. They

– the sheep (for example) who live with me; the sheep I live with – out-pace me; they are stronger than I; and yet I am I. The other day I fell, at the door of the writing-room, was pushed off-balance, unintentionally, by one of the sheep coming out of that room (a visit) and within a second was face-down on the soil outside, with them grazing about me. The vast human world, all its culture and intellect, understanding, is a mere bubble. Its skin is so thin that it can burst at any moment and you are there, face-down, in the soil, unable to get up. One learns – hopefully one learns! – a respect for it, the soil, as a far more abiding thing.

12
Dying, Perishing [5]

Martin Heidegger is widely considered one of the key philosophers of the twentieth century. A Nazi sympathiser and long-time member of the party – a man who, when it counted, failed to support Edmund Husserl, his own mentor, because Husserl was Jewish – he is also one of the most controversial. Author of *Being and Time* (1927) and *The Fundamental Concepts of Metaphysics* (1983: in fact a lecture course he'd given in 1929/30), he's the author, too, of one of the most troublesome statements about non-human animals made by a major philosopher since Déscartes.

Deeply troubled by the 'animal' aspect of human being (he wrote, in his 'Letter on Humanism' in 1946, of our 'scarcely fathomable, abyssal bodily kinship with the animal'), Heidegger went to great lengths trying to separate the two, although the non-human animal he distinguishes the human from can't be seen, it seems to me, as much more than a *paper* animal, a non-existent composite of things Heidegger doesn't want the human to be. Humans can experience 'Da-sein' – *Being* in an intense, existential form. Animals – his *imagined* animals – can't.

The aforementioned statement, that 'humans die, animals *perish*' (emphasis mine), is in fact the final in a sequence of three deeply interrelated declarations, each of which could be described as, at best, perplexing, at worst scurrilous, even heinous.

The first statement of this group – to the effect that 'the going-out-of-the-world of Dasein in the sense of dying must be distinguished from a going-out-of-the-world of what is only alive', appeared in *Being and Time*.[6] 'The ending of what is only alive', the statement continues, 'we formulate terminologically as *perishing*' (again, my emphasis).

The second and most notorious of the three – phrased so oddly he might almost be able, were he at that time, on that spot, called to account, to say that he did *not* say it ('Ah, but that is not what I *meant......*')[7] – occurred twenty-two years later, during a lecture in Bremen on December 1st 1949[8], and was to the effect that those who were murdered in Nazi extermination camps did not *die*, but only *perished*:

> Hundreds of thousands die *en masse*. Do they die? They perish. They become items of the standing reserve for the manufacture of corpses. Do they die? Hardly noticed they are liquidated in extermination camps.... Dying, however, means

bearing death in its essence. To be capable of dying means to be capable of bearing this death. But we are able to do so only when the essence of death has an affinity to our essence.[9]

It should perhaps be noted that this was in fact the second reference to concentration camp victims made by Heidegger that day. In a lecture a few hours earlier he had likened them to the victims of industrial farming. 'Agriculture', he'd said,

is now a mechanized food industry. As for its essence, it is the same thing as the manufacture of corpses in the gas chambers and the death camps, the same thing as the blockades and reduction of countries to famine, the same thing as the manufacture of hydrogen bombs.[10]

Three statements, then, very similar, informing and elaborating one another. That those who experience Dasein *die*, whereas those who 'only live' *perish*; that those who were slaughtered 'industrially' (like the victims of industrial farming), did not *die*, but merely *perished*; and that *humans* die, *animals* perish.

It might be tempting, with regard to the second of these statements, to think that Heidegger may be using the word *perish* to try to mitigate something of the appalling horror of the gas chambers. That is, that he's attempting to reduce the severity of the experience that their victims underwent in the sudden termination of their lives by suggesting that that very suddenness somehow changed the nature of that experience, that termination.

Elsewhere, however, and somewhat earlier, Heidegger appears to have ruled out such a gambit. *Dying*, he argues in *Being and Time*, is a quite different thing from 'perishing', a fuller consciousness of the process one is going through as one's life approaches its close. We must look at this fuller consciousness, what it entails, and why Heidegger should have spent so much ink upon it.

The moment and mode of death seem crucial to Heidegger's distinction of the human from the non-human animal. The moment of death and the process of dying are where the conceptual (dis-animalised) human and the human *animal* come together – so *closely* together, indeed, one might almost think them inseparable. For a philosopher who's been so concerned to *separate* them, it becomes, therefore, a very crucial moment/process indeed, a moment and process where his powers of separation – his ability to sustain, intellectually, that separation – are most severely tested. It would be so easy, in the *extremis* of death, to succumb to the *animal*. The mind must be prepared, strengthened, to survive this crisis. The *non*-animal human, in the process of death, must resist the human animal with all its/his/her force.

Heidegger's attempts to articulate the mode of this preparation would appear to be indebted to a stance Rilke had already proposed, in his *Sonnets to Orpheus* (and Wallace Stevens, on the other side of the Atlantic, in such poems as 'Sunday Morning' [1923]); that is, that we should orient ourselves toward and attempt to assimilate our own death well before it happens, as a means of intensifying our experience of life ('be ahead of all parting,' Rilke writes, 'as though it already were behind you'[11]).

Humans, Heidegger argues, might not be aware of death in this way *throughout* their lives – they might have a period early in those lives when they've not yet begun to experience such fore-shadowing – but, from the moment they become aware of it, they live, as it were, in death's ante-chamber, with the knowledge and anticipation that death will eventually come. A knowledge and anti-cipation which add to the life which precedes it that which at once separates that life from that of those who are 'only living', and enables it to resist, in the moment of death itself, one's succumbing to the animal. In his initial formulation it is the fore-shadow, not the moment/mode of the death, upon which the distinction between *dying* and *perishing* turns. The *anticipation* – this fore-shadow – is, for Heidegger, paramount.

Of course, in an *instantaneous* experience of one's life's ending, such as might occur if one is run over by a bus, expires of a heart attack in one's sleep, or finds that the shower-head is not giving forth water but a choking gas – i.e. an experience/realisation that that process has actually begun, such as may take the form of one's not having realised/'known' this in one moment, but have realised/'known' it in the next – it is hard to see how one might have the chance to recall and sustain such preparations. It is just as hard, however, to see how one could say categorically that people who die in this sudden manner have not had the chance to commence and even advance such preparations, or to have their lives in some measure enriched/intensified by so doing. One experiences the death of others and anticipates – fore-contemplates – one's own; one lies awake in the pitch dark and anticipates – experiences – the horror of non-being; one lies in a sickbed and wonders whether one will survive the illness. And indeed Heidegger, right from the start, would seem to have covered this, with the injection of a third term. 'Da-sein, too,' he says

> can end without authentically dying, though on the other hand, qua Da-sein, it does not simply perish. We call this inter-mediate phenomenon its *demise*.[12]

With the exception, it seems, of the shower-head. When, in the Bremen lecture, *withholding* this third option, he writes that those whose lives are ended 'industrially' in the extermination camps do not *die*, but *perish*, we have little choice but to conclude that he is either (a) insisting that *these* people are in some way *not* human (are 'only living', are *animals* perhaps, to look to the first and third iterations), or (b) that they have never, before these instants of their death, entered death's ante-chamber, i.e. that *these* people have never thought of death's coming, have never lain awake at night in anguish at the apprehension of their own eventual extinction, and so forth. Either of which, regarding a living human, is a despicable position to take, and for a philosopher – but this is such a tiny point by comparison – such poor thinking one wonders how one has come to be accepted as such in the first place.

But the point of my discussing this here and now, of course, is that he says it, a year later, in an essay on Rilke ('The Thing' in 1950), about animals: that humans *die*, but animals merely *perish*. We can hardly be surprised; 'animals' have been implicit all along, the separation *from* them fundamental to the presentation of Dasein in the first place.

Heaven forbid, then, that non-human animals be found, *as they can so readily be found*, to have rituals of death; heaven forbid that non-human animals be found to grieve, that non-human animals be found to have their own modes of preparation *for* death. Heaven forbid, especially, that non-human animals might, in their own, non-human ways, find their lives enriched by a foreshadowing of death.

But this of course, in his attempts to sequestrate the human, is Heidegger's Achilles heel: that he does not consult *actual* non-human animals, who might have contradicted him, but sets up a paper/conceptual 'animal' to separate his (paper/conceptual) human from, an animal whose distinctive features are not so much features of actual non-human animals, as features which do not suit Heidegger's image of the human, and proceeds to tell us – something that, by his own admission (our 'scarcely fathomable, abyssal bodily kinship with the animal'), he finds virtually unknowable – what is and what is not in the 'animal' mind.

13
On the Separation of 'Life' and 'Work'

I've seen it stated that a separation of life and work – the philosopher's (auto)*biography* from his/her *writing* – is a wide-spread assumption of Continental Philosophy. I'm not so sure, but the division is familiar enough. Certainly Heidegger, perhaps unsurprisingly, makes it something of a cornerstone, and we find it enduring in the opinions of such of his followers as Jacques Derrida. What is my problem with this? Why do I feel, for example, that some consideration of Derrida's eating habits and his attitude toward vegetarianism are pertinent to an assessment of his self-proclaimed 'animal turn'? Is it just the apparent hypocrisy of it – that a philosopher can advocate, can ask us to believe them about, modes of being and behaviour that have so little convinced them that they themselves don't feel obliged to follow them (for surely, in choosing themselves to ignore them, they give tacit permission for everyone else to ignore them also) – or might it be something more? How could it be that we reach such a predicament, where a philosopher can't abide by his/her own thinking? Is it possible, perhaps, that these two things – the Animal, and the lived life – are somehow strangely, bizarrely, allied, as *outsides* of philosophy?

Why *is* it that 'the life' cannot conform to 'the work' (in this case 'the philosophy')? It may – I'm not sure that it always is – be absolutely true that it can't, but in that case where does the problem lie, and aren't we indulging in a rather critical intellectual laziness in leaving the matter there? Is the intransigence – what else to call it? *that which will not adapt to the other*? – in the life, or in the philosophy? It will be widely argued, of course, that philosophy all along has dealt with ideals, not with the vicissitudes of mundane being, but is this really adequate? Isn't there therefore a kind of conceptual deficit? A challenge not being taken up? Wouldn't philosophy be the better if it pushed itself through that murky barrier, over that difficult terrain, didn't allow itself to be content until it could somehow speak, and work to integrate, the languages of both places?

14
Light-heartedness

The predicament of the non-human animal at this stage of the Anthropocene is critical and horrific and it's unconscionable it be treated with anything other than the utmost seriousness. But mightn't we be missing something – *not yet arriving* at something – if we allow that seriousness to become our only or our dominant mode? Must we, even as we seek to aid and liberate such non-human animals as much as we find ourselves able to, bring them into the grey dome of our own mental/intellectual/moral winter? We might not be doing more harm that way, but could we be limiting what we *can* do? Are we *learning* what we can? *To allow ourselves to be led*: what would/does that feel like?

I see my wife's spirits rise – a *visible*, *palpable* thing – as she goes down to the sheep, just as I see theirs rise as she approaches. And I have seen something similar – I want to call it the *same* thing – in so many other animal rescue workers. A *lightening in them* as they approach. A lightening, no doubt, that is dismissed by those unsympathetic to what they do – or perhaps those just unsympathetic, period – as a sort of simple-mindedness. And yet I know it to be anything but. Indeed I'm speaking of some of the most complex and competent minds I know. Perhaps they already know, in this regard, the kind of knowledge (wisdom?) I'm reaching for. Or perhaps it's a Gift, of that rare kind that makes the Gifted a giver, a source of supply. The lightness – light-*hearted*ness – surely then has its place, may even (here's a thought) be an affect *of* place.

15
On Learning to See

Nietzsche's *The Twilight of the Idols* was completed at Sils Maria just before he packed his bags for Turin, and was published soon after his breakdown. Here's an intriguing passage:

Learning to see – habituating the eye to repose, to patience, to letting things come to it; learning to defer judgement, to investigate and comprehend the individual case in all its aspects. This is the *first* preliminary schooling in spirituality: *not* to react immediately to a stimulus, but to have the restraining, stock-taking instincts in one's control. Learning to *see* … is almost what is called in unphilosophical language 'strong will-power': the essence of it is precisely *not* to 'will', the *ability* to defer decision.… A practical application of having learned to see: one will have become slow, mistrustful, resistant as a *learner* in general. In an attitude of hostile calm one will allow the strange, the *novel* of every kind to approach one first – one will draw one's hand back from it.[13]

Such delicate and cautious passages – calls for restraint, in our acts of perception, upon our overweening Human presumption – do sometimes occur in Nietzsche. One of my favourites is from *Dawn* (1881), where he writes of reading 'slowly, deeply, looking cautiously before and aft, with reservations, with doors left open, with delicate eyes and fingers…'.[14]

16
Dark Places

In any negotiation between opposing political or military forces (Russian and Ukrainian; Israeli and Palestinian; Tamil and Sinhalese, etc.), there are, it seems, places it's not advisable for negotiators to go, issues it isn't wise to raise. Similarly, whenever different *ethoi* or *regimes of thought* are brought into close contact – as, for example, that which sustains itself upon the oppression and instrumentalisation of non-human animals (based upon a belief that the world is *about* and *for* the human animal), and that which seeks their liberation from such instrumentalisation – there are dark places, holes, pockets of radical and potentially disruptive incompatibility. After all, we can't expect that their coastlines, like pieces in a jig-saw puzzle, will be a perfect match.

I've written already (*Where does it stop?*) of two of these – the issues of sentience, and of whether and where we might draw a clear line between what we can and cannot eat – and of my being advised (the Argument to Silence) to stay clear of such issues because to raise them, if only to criticise those who've failed to respond to or explain them adequately, is to expose the fact that there may not *be* clear answers to or explanations of them, and so, supposedly, to weaken the argument for animals overall.

Elsewhere I've discussed – again, against advice not to go there – the troublesome paradox that, if one saves a human life, then one is potentially, if the person one saves is not vegan, ensuring the death of a large number of other, non-human animals.

Elsewhere, too, I've spoken of the contentiousness of likening the situation of non-human animals, both within the industrial farming system and otherwise, to the Holocaust or Shoah, as if it is somehow deeply inappropriate to compare the suffering of non-human and human animals, as if it's not possible that non-human animals can suffer as much as human animals, and as if the comparison was not first made, and has not been frequently supported, by victim-survivors of the Holocaust themselves.

It's not as if one doesn't understand some of the pressure to silence, on these and on many other such matters. With any advance in our thinking the animal comes the corresponding fear, for example, that our findings will be turned, ultimately, to the benefit of *homo omnicidens* (killer of everything) – that, instead of an opening (of mind, of being) *to* non-human beings, there will be *colonisation*, use – and a corresponding suspicion that we should remain silent, or at least circumspect, about what we have been privileged to experience or discover. Mere attention, at times, can seem a form of damage. But on the other hand the monstrous behaviour and massive ignorance of so many humans toward non-human animals must be protested and counteracted by all means possible, and one feels just as strongly – hopes – that some exposure to the deeper lives of non-humans might just turn a tide of opinion away from instrumentalisation and toward their favour and protection.

As for the fear that discussing openly some of the logical and logistical problems we encounter may reveal some deep *il*logicality within our ('animalist'?) position and so expose the entire project to ridicule and rejection, might it not be that if we cannot resolve the attendant questions *reasonably*, as in by use of reason, that the fault is not so much in ourselves, as in the reason we are asked for or feel we have to employ? *That* reason, one is tempted to say, has much of its governance in philosophy and its time-honoured systems of logic, and for millennia these have not only turned their back upon non-human animals, but formed a phalanx against them.

We can't, in any case, close down these and other such questions by turning *our* backs upon them. We *must* think 'the question of the Animal'. The thinking of the question – in *all* its aspects – is integral to the liberation of non-human animals (or, if that aspiration is too precipitate, to the swiftest and most effective redress of their suffering). Even if, as I suspect we might, we ultimately dismiss some of the difficult, seemingly irresolvable questions we encounter as generated by the wrong paradigm, we must be able to explain this – I might almost go a step further and say explain this *in the terms of* that wrong paradigm. Despite Kant's (in this respect) relatively *uncritical* *Critique of Pure Reason*, might it not be, after all, that there *is* no such thing as 'pure' reason (or at least, and this *is* a point of Kant's, that there is not as much 'pure' reason as we are led to believe)?

There are different paradigms, different regimes of thought, and all such different paradigms and regimes produce, and employ, their own 'reason' (or variant of reason, if that's how you'd have it). We have, in a sense, *choices* of reason(s), each of which, if we can term a central logos or ethos an 'affect' on a large scale, is *affected* or *affect-driven*. And if our affect is co-existential and compassionate, rather than domineering and instrumentalising, then, although we might have a mighty load of work to do to articulate *its* logic, *its* reason, we should nevertheless knuckle down to it.

17

Getting Over Ourselves

A man just came by who's been doing some work for us and, charmed again by the sheep, mentioned he's been telling his children about them, and they're asking him if they can 'have' sheep. He lives on five acres further down the mountain and has the space; you can tell he's as interested as they are. But I'm not sure I trust him to take only – to *wait* for – 'rescue' sheep. I suspect, if he and his family decide to 'have' sheep, he's more likely to go out and buy a couple from some farmer nearby.

From one angle that's just not on. One rescues sheep when one can, but one doesn't *buy* them, since this only supports the industry. Any sheep taken out of the system in this manner will be swiftly replaced.

Should this man be discouraged then? It's not as simple a question as it appears.

On the one hand there's a chance any sheep we *rescue* will be replaced just as readily, and arguably neither of us, rescuers or purchasers, are making much difference. But on the other we *are*, each of us, saving some lives, and, although we cannot hope to change the culture of millennia overnight or even in our lifetimes, we can't discount – daren't, for in some ways it's one of the few things we have – the possibility that the example we set, of choosing to let live, to befriend and help rather than master, exploit and devour, will have, cumu-latively, some effect. One of the children of this man may decide that he or she will not eat meat, because of the sheep he or she has known. Or a friend might. The man himself might. The odds are against these things – the countervailing pressure is intense and relentless – but they're much worse if we do nothing.

A lot of the time we can barely see the effects of our actions and lifestyles, but what kind of effects will we see if we *don't* do what we are doing? T. asked me, numerous times, in darker moments, in our first years, what the point was in all our advocacy: we didn't see changes, or saw only minor ones. In three or four years we could point to no friend or acquaintance who'd become vegan. But now, another five years on – friends, acquaintances, students – we can think of a dozen.

Whether such things have anything in particular to do with any one of us is anybody's guess. Few of us have any idea what effect our choices and lifestyles and actions and practices have on others; but (a) if we truly believe in them we will do them regardless; they will be unconditional and won't in any way depend upon visible successes or credit to ourselves, and (b) if we *don't* do them – if we give up because we can't see evidence of our effects upon others – we give tacit permission for everyone else to give up also, and then where would we be? More importantly, where would so many non-human animals be?

In some ways our own patience, commitment and – I was going to say persistence, but I think *consistency* is the better word – are some of the best devices we have. In some vital senses we don't know who we are – that's for others to decide –

and the desire to see the positive effects of our actions and examples, the desire to be *rewarded* in this way, might ultimately be irrelevant and, worse, counterproductive. In this, as in so many other ways, we must get over ourselves. We are not *doing* this for ourselves.

18

Possession

V.S., leaning across a table in the saloon bar of The Black Bull, Toronto, 1977: *Nothing is possessed until it is articulated*, meaning, as I took it then and was profoundly struck by, that we can't claim – don't in fact 'possess' – a thought, haven't really *got hold of it*, until we can *say* it clearly and unambiguously. By extrapolation, if we find we can't articulate a thought or idea clearly in this way then we need to go back and do some more work on it, *get it straight*.

Right. A Wittgensteinian legacy, clearly. *The limits of my world are the limits of my language.* And part of me still believes this, within fairly strict limits. But just as much a part is in another camp – probably was there already even as I heard V.S. speak those words, though it's been a long time coming clear, getting straight. That Nothing – as a *place*, a *realm*, that Mallarmé knew something of, say, or Rilke when he wrote of the Open, or myself now as I try so tentatively, paradoxically, *impossibly* to 'enter' the world of animals, if only by asserting and accepting that it exists – is possessed only *until* it is articulated, at which point – when it *is* articulated – while it does not necessarily cease to exist, it slips *from* possession, *articulation* having meant that it's been drawn into the realm of language and so, to borrow Blanchot's cartoon-like simplification – or perhaps just make it seem cartoon-like in the borrowing – has become a dead thing.

But it's *so hard*, I find – the real point here – to *let go* of language; indeed it's something akin to an existential crisis: to allow oneself entry to and credit to oneself the existence of that realm beyond language; to control – in fact deny to oneself – that obsessive need to name and explain and 'understand' what one is feeling or experiencing, indeed that need even to know, without its attendant language, that one is being or experiencing at all.

19

The Human Animal Consumed

I've never been able to track down the place where the great Portuguese poet Fernando Pessoa states that the pressure to cohere is one of the madnesses of our times. Perhaps he didn't say it at all. Nevertheless it seemed so right, wherever and however I encountered it, that it's stayed with me for decades now, a kind of truism.

This pressure to cohere – this pressure to be *individual*, to be *integral*, that is one of the madnesses of our times (or one of the things that *drives* us mad) – is arguably of fairly recent origin. According to Foucault and others, it began with the industrial revolution and has been coeval with our eventual/current saturation capitalism.[15] The desire to be individual, and to mark oneself out as such through the purchase of objects which serve to signify one's particular character, fashions one as consumerism's subject – consumerism depending upon and so constantly shaping and stimulating this desire – and therefore, of course, as its victim. One focusses upon one's self; one ornaments that self with appropriate clothing, possessions, behaviours, etc., so as to pronounce, articulate and emphasise one's difference. One is therefore not only *divided from others*, and in this extent politically disenfranchised, but the very process one is led to think makes one stand out *from* the culture may in fact only be making one serve it the better. As we are led to think we are escaping we may in fact be being lured, as it were, *to* the slaughter – *consumed* as we consume – in a manner strangely comparable to the non-human animals we insist be raised to be consumed by us.

Am I then making a critique of individuality? Hardly. But I am, I think, cautioning that in pursuing one's self and determining one's purposes, desires and goals, one must be aware of this double face, this trap, and do what one can to avoid it.

20
Collateral

I am weeding an onion-grass-infested bed in the vegetable garden, approaching a new stand of the clover-tipped sprouts, pushing the trowel deep into the soil beneath, to try to get all the pink-white corms, when a spider appears from the neighbouring clump, one of those garden spiders with a large white abdomen that looks like a miniature ping-pong ball.

It must be that the earth has literally shifted beneath her feet. She leaves the weed forest – to her it must seem just that, a tall, protective forest – and clambers up a hill nearby, in a suddenly-devastated landscape, which is to say makes her way up a small ridge of soil, six or seven centimetres high, at the edge of the area I've already cleared, but then pauses and (it's as if I can *see* what she's thinking) decides she's too exposed there and heads back to shelter in a different part of the onion-grass forest, a little to the north of the clump I've just disturbed.

The mind *goes to* the spider. She is briefly 'I', 'I' briefly her. 'Traditional', 'accepted' thought will almost certainly *not* accept this, has bulwarks against such intrusions, but one cannot allow these any sway, for all their supposed normality, *because* of that normality. They're tainted ground. A little later, still in my garden, I lift a brick, and expose – disturb – a colony of ants. I can carefully put the brick back into place, but how many ants will I kill or injure in so doing? I'm damned if I do, it seems, and damned if I don't. What else have I ruptured or destroyed?

Later still, in a different part of the garden, going at a weed-mass with a hoe (there's been such heat and rain; the weeds are everywhere), I see a ladybug crawling along a long blade of grass, away from my disturbance. Doubtless she is one of many. And there will be, down in the soil I've just turned, slaters, other spiders, ants, millipedes, centipedes, earthworms, grubs, more creatures than I can possibly name. Even up in the house, later, as I wash the lettuce leaves I've just collected, there are two tiny slugs, and an earwig trying desperately to stay afloat. I lift them up carefully on a spoon, take them outside.

Collateral. There seems to be collateral damage to almost every action, in almost everything one does. No matter how careful and caring one wishes or tries to be. What consideration to give to this? What weight? Where does it sit, in our talk of ethics, animal rights? Where – at what animal, which insect – do *those* rights cease? Does an ant have one millionth of the life of a human, or is every life the same? If we believe a life *is* a life, how can we make exceptions? And yet, merely walking, we kill.

We must move with such care. The Jains faced this problem centuries ago, declared they would eat no animal, vertebrate or invertebrate, mammal or insect. Jain priests, I'm told, walk with a broom, to sweep the path before them so that they don't step on an ant. Their policy of *ahimsa* (non-violence) one's highest religious duty: *all souls support one another, one must kill no living being, large or small.* How then do *they* get through their days? To *intend* to kill another being, even a mosquito, let alone to kill it deliberately, is a serious sin. But there is a caveat: it is a not-so-serious sin, a *forgivable* sin, if one kills *un*intentionally, in the course of performing the processes and functions necessary to one's life: cooking, washing, walking about (working, earning money), and provided one takes due care in performing those processes and functions. Eat during the day (there is more danger to insects when one cooks at night). Wear mouth-cover. *Cover standing liquids* to avoid drowning insects. And mindfulness, always mindfulness.

I'm not sure they have it. It's still a *compelled* compassion, with enticements – one observes the rituals for the protection and advancement of one's own soul, not first and foremost just out of a clear and entirely voluntary recognition and respect for animal others. And it's still a hierarchy: five-sensed beings at the top (five-sensed + mind [humans] at the apex), then four-sensed, three-sensed, etc., the more senses a being has (supposedly) the more that being feels pain, therefore the more it should be protected and respected (a touch Benthamite/ utilitarian here: 'can it *suffer?*').

Still, the covering of standing water makes sense. And to keep thinking.

21
The Impossible Contract

Condescension. The conviction of innate superiority. Another of the dark places. More than one animal rights advocate has at some point declared that they don't feel the need to shift from their vegetarianism to veganism because the animals we've saved from slaughter or whose circumstances as producers we've managed to improve nevertheless and consequentially *owe* us. This may in some part be generational – things are changing, and there would seem to be less and less people adopting such a position – but it exists as a position and requires examination nevertheless.

The point implies a *contractual* arrangement. While there can be no assumption that a contract is fair or evenly balanced – the vast majority of contracts between humans probably are not – the basis of contract is that both parties *to* a contract are aware of what that contract is, and aware that they are entering into it. No such contract exists, or could exist, with the non-human animals we exploit and force to suffer for our consumption; indeed I think it's true to say, contract being an exclusive preoccupation of the *human* animal, no contract is possible with a *non*-human animal in the first place.

Consuming the products of animal suffering at the same time as campaigning to reduce that suffering. What goes on in the human mind to allow such contradiction? Either there is a *cognitive dissonance* between one's dietary habits and one's knowledge and understanding of animal exploitation and suffering, or one has contrived – has found – an excuse or explanation to give oneself for the manner in which one's dietary habits appear in direct contradiction to this knowledge and understanding.

In the case of people who are not in the first place animal rights workers and/or advocates, the first may be a possibility. In the case of animal rights workers and advocates, however, who so frequently not only face but deplore such suffering and its link to dietary habits, it can only be the latter, in which case they are either caught in and quite conscious of a flagrant hypocrisy, or they feel they have a *right* to eat as they do.

Again, it's the latter that is most probable. And for this felt/assumed right there would seem to be only two clear possible explanations. If we invite, at its 'settled' extreme, welfarism into the equation – and holding aside its turning, as it does, upon the grotesque myth of 'humane' slaughter – there's the possibility that they feel that where animals *have* an improved quality of life, when they have been brought up as *humanely* as possible, where they have suffered as little as possible, then they are, in a sense, there to be instrumentalised for dietary purposes. But – some wilful occlusion notwithstanding – it would seem likely that animal rights advocates would know too much to have allowed themselves this course, and that the more likely explanation is a simpler one: that, having *rescued* and/or *helped improve the quality of life* of so many animals, they have *earned the right*, albeit in moderation, to eat as they wish. ('If I have helped save so many chickens, then surely even the chickens themselves would allow me a few eggs, a few mouthfuls of flesh.' 'If I have fought so hard for the rights of cows and their calves, then surely they would not begrudge me a little milk, a little of the cheese made from it.'[16])

Work, then, and effort, seen as a matter of a *giving* from those who have to those who have not, with something of the dark economy of the gift. Charity, condescension, compassion, for which some reward might be expected. Rather, say, than a matter of recognition and respect for an inherent right that a fellow creature has. Like so many of our other interactions with animals, the aid extended seen as *conditional* and *transactional*. A sense of effort-leading-to-reward that ghosts, with contract, so many of our animal interactions. A hang-over from that conventional economy that occasions the mass enslavement and persecution of animals in the first place, to say nothing of the system of virtue and reward about which mass religions turn.

But the reward is *taken*, not given. No *human* animal would tolerate or accept such a one-sided contract except under duress, a duress that in many cases and places would, legally, invalidate the contract in the first place. We must therefore assume that the animal's tacit acceptance of such a contract, if we allow it as any acceptance at all – but how could we? – is tantamount to acceptance-under-duress. We are deciding upon this 'contract' *on the animals' behalf*, and assuming – *arrogating* to ourselves – the right to do so, a matter at once of power-relation and intellectual violence, a regressive and lethal extension of the very assumption of superiority and dominion that the animal rights and liberation movements have claimed for so long to be fighting to undo.

*

This conditionality and *transactionality* infiltrate the very minutiae of our interrelations with the non-human animals about us. Even those interrelations we might think the most benign. The very movements we make, I think sometimes, as we attempt, physically, to approach a non-human animal. A whole regime of intrusive gesture – touch, gaze, sound, smell, and more – that unwittingly hardens the air and cruels the space between us despite the tenderest intentions. The softest caress that, strange and uncomfortable, can also be a *holding away*. Why do we need it? Why is so much, in our modes of approach, still about *us*? That extending of our arms that, benign as it may be, cannot but recall those other humans who have done so only in the process of abusing: of catching, confining, marking, docking, cutting into flesh, forcing unpalatable concoctions down throats.

We move down to the rescued sheep (pigs, cows, ducks, horses…), extend our hands through the fence, reach out. But the mere expectation of response, let alone gratitude – the cores of the impossible contract – is an extension of our own face and desire. *Nothing that we give, nothing that we do, obliges them to us*. Until we can manage to get over such expectations, that face and desire will obscure all that, in our encounters with other animals, we think we see. It's only in the *fading* of that face – in our training ourselves out of such expectations – that we will begin to see the face of the other, and that those deeply compromised things we might like to think of as our gifts to them (our charity, our compassion) may give way to respect.

22

Animal Dreams

The brains of sheep are so like the brains of us human animals. For all their *un*likeness. The brains of sheep, the brains of horses, the brains of dogs, the brains of ducks, the brains of kangaroos. Reasonable to think, then, that *their* dream-work might be like *our* dream work. It would be hard, given all we know about their brain structure, to think it's not: that, unlike *our* brains, *their* brains are empty, inactive, blank from the moment they fall asleep to the moment they wake again.

We once thought – many still do – that dreams predict the future, or that they're evidence we live also in worlds other than the waking one, or that they're the past coming to visit us, summoned by correspondences we mightn't realise and certainly can't control: new anxieties calling up ancient ones, new griefs and expectations and challenges dragging up old, etc. Current wisdom, backed by science (which in itself might be seen as a kind of dream), is that the brain, during *our* sleep, settles and re-orders itself after the day's activity, much as a computer reboots, and that our dreams are a part of this process.

How can we possibly maintain that the brains of *non*-human animals don't do something similar? Or that, waking from a dream-state, a sheep, a hyena, a kangaroo, a snake, a rat, a magpie won't sometimes find themself, just as we do, carrying fragments of their dreams into the waking day? Do *they* dream of things from their past? Surely they must. Do *they* dream of others they know? Surely they must. Does Henry the sheep, for example, dream of Jonathan the sheep? Does Jonathan dream of Orpheus? Does Orpheus the sheep see his dead mother in his dreams? Do Henry and Jonathan re-encounter their old friends Mabel and

Sookie? Does Jason have nightmares about his time in the swamp behind the brickworks? Impossible, of course, to answer any such questions definitively, but does the impossibility of answering a question definitively mean the question doesn't *have* answers? And if there are dream-lives, dream worlds, then surely there are going to be attempts, on the part of the kangaroo, the horse, the snake, the sheep, to explain them to themselves.

How do they do that?

23
The Work of Undoing

A paradoxical situation. We feel such diffidence, presumption and awkwardness in approaching the worlds of non-human animals, and yet we too are animals. Humankind has worked for so many thousands of years to build this barrier between itself and other creatures, to suppress and occlude and discount the animal within ourselves, that *is* ourselves, and now there is this immense work of undoing…

24

The Burden of the Other

...but while the acknowledgement and re-admission of *our* 'animal other' is of indisputable significance we must take care it doesn't obscure the even greater question of what we can and must do *for* non-human animals, or impose in any way a further burden upon them. The burden of the other is entirely our own.

If *in our eyes* there is an otherness in non-human animals, the largest part of it is because we've done something *to* our eyes. There is the work, then, of undoing, but also, surely, some possibility of training ourselves to see more clearly. The very concept of otherness is a barrier. Emphasising *difference*,[17] it obscures *similarity*.

Does it occur to us, when we propose this otherness, that if, rather than thinking of the animal as *concept*, we were to spend *actual* time with *actual* non-human animals, some of the 'other' in those animals might *articulate*, come to seem less and less so; that at least some of the othering – *this* face of the othering – may be an effect of distance and ignorance in the first place? That the 'other', observed, *experienced*, may become something *other than itself*? That knowledge is an effect of *relation* (or, rather, that an effect of relation is knowledge)?

25
A Sad Story

An ecologist friend nearly three years ago led an extensive and, to my thinking, heroic relocation of kangaroos from a site where, had they remained, they'd have been culled – murdered – or scattered by the local council, who were intent on destroying the orchard in which they lived. Week after week, month after month, five or six or seven kangaroos per night (it had to be done at night), all carried out with the utmost care and under veterinary supervision, a project initially strongly supported by the national wildlife service, who promised an expedited permit, but who subsequently delayed the project and imposed so many conditions upon it that one can't but think their intention was to stall matters to the point where the kangaroos would be shot and the business done with. Had there been a power-shift within the wildlife service? Had my friend trodden on somebody's toes? The service has long claimed the relocation of kangaroos is not a viable option. Had someone decided they couldn't allow this to be tested?

With almost super-human effort, and at great personal expense to all involved, all but two of the kangaroos were relocated successfully. Well over two years later, my friend still tortures himself over the pair who didn't survive, their femurs fractured by the impact of the dart. ('There is a fragile bone in the middle of the target area,' he tells me, 'subject to sudden stresses as the animal bunches its muscles to leap, the angle of incidence a part of it. There's popping noise. The animal lurches away on one leg in the dark.') It's pointless to try to shift his attention to the hundreds he and his volunteers managed to rescue. Despite their having stipulated a mortality rate of less than 20% (in fact it was less than half of *one* percent), and threatening to prosecute him for 'harming' the kangaroos he'd moved, once word got out amongst the local kangaroo shooters that there were now relocated kangaroos around the release area, the authorities readily handed out permits to shoot them, and shooters themselves turned it into a competition, posting pictures of the killing to social media.

Kangaroos, of course, are just one set of victims amongst many in our perennial war against non-humans, but they are persecuted so viciously and paradoxically (they're also an icon, a national emblem, provide the names of many of our national teams, etc.) that they seem to focalise something beyond themselves – are scapegoats, I've sometimes thought, for the hatred many humans still don't feel quite free to express toward one another, or toward the animal in themselves. But in truth this hatred has numerous sources. We've mistreated animals for so long, and the guilt at this mistreatment has festered within us so long, that – counterintuitively, against all 'reason' – animals themselves are being held to blame for being there to be mistreated in the first place.

We look around ourselves, in times of drought, at the desolated landscape, and blame kangaroos for the lack of grass; it doesn't seem to factor that it's the sheep and cattle we've put there who've eaten most of it, and that the devastation's been caused by our own attitudes, our own malpractice. Now we settlers are dependent upon this devastated ground for our livelihood, and the roos are still there, survivors, witnesses to our impotence and error. Our embarrassment knows no bounds. Someone has to be to blame; someone has to be the subject of the rage and frustration. And it seems the roos are it. The designated protectors of our wildlife do almost nothing. The killers are encouraged. Administrative corruption goes unchecked. Those who save lives are ridiculed, punished and persecuted, and carry on their backs, because they care, burdens almost too great to bear.

26
Tribes

Foolish to think we could ever have an end to hierarchy and distinction, the division which conquers, so take this, rather, as challenge. That we see ourselves as tribes, of the one being. A point brought home so simply by a story I heard yesterday. A friend, some years ago, went up into the roof-space of his house in Sydney to investigate a smell, thought to be a dead possum. He found not one dead possum but dozens, the *skeletons* of dozens, carefully lined up in rows as if in a graveyard ('no *as if:* it *was* a graveyard'). It was not my friend himself but his wife who told me the tale. They'd had problems with possums in the roof for some time and had earlier had a man come in to trap and remove them. This he'd done, and had taken them to a park some ten minutes away. But within a few days, she said, the possums had returned. This was their *spirit* ground, she said, with a kind of awe in her voice: these were the graves of their *ancestors*.

27

A Tragic Mistake

Day after day I'm more conscious of the mind I'm not using, the being I'm not becoming, the vast spaces, here, now, that I'm not entering, can't find the key to. As if something were up to *me*, but what? And how could this be? The whole of human endeavour, for centuries, millennia, lingering on this edge? But how could *that* be? Some days, though I look into the mirror, it seems even my own face is not visible to me, and I think that there has been a tragic mistake, thinking that *being* was so much about *knowing*.

28

Notes on the Discard

Supermarkets must by law discard items that have passed their use-by dates or, when then discounted, have not been sold within a certain period. They must also discard damaged items, or items that, regardless of date, have become stale, show signs of mould, begun to rot, etc. I'm told that, at my local supermarket, a box of two dozen bottles (of soy or tomato sauce, say) may be thrown out if one bottle is broken, not so much because the contents of that bottle will have stained the rest, as because staff might cut themselves on the broken glass, an occupational health and safety matter.

Often these discarded items are placed in large bins outside the supermarket for regular municipal garbage collections. A great deal of quite edible, largely harmless food is disposed of in this way. To 'dumpster dive' is to scavenge in these bins for such items, in order to provide for or supplement one's diet. A Freegan I heard interviewed recently claimed forty percent of his diet came from this practice.

What is the ethical status of such discarded items? In a sense they enter a space of abjection. Do the ethics concerning those items while on supermarket shelves still apply in the space of the discard, or are they somehow suspended? Is one obliged to maintain one's own ethics, in a space where they have no tangible effect?

The utilisation of the discard often reflects a conscious reluctance to participate in what we might term the 'conventional' economy. To *purchase* an item is to register and/or create or sustain, if not a *need* for that item, then at least a *market* for it. Until an item is discarded, to relieve the supermarket of that item without paying for it is classified as theft and people caught so doing are subject to significant penalties. The moment the item is discarded, however, such penalties and classifications cease to apply, and one may be free to take it.

For a *vegan* interested in such items the situation is less clear. A vegan does not eat anything that can be deemed the product of animal suffering, not only because it *is* the product of such suffering, but also because to purchase and consume such products is to support the industries and markets sustaining such suffering. If one's not *purchasing* these products, however – if one is instead encountering them as *discard* – is one then free to eat them? Has their ethical status changed in this respect also? Might one even, in some manner, be *obliged* to eat them?

An argument exists that to discard such items, after the suffering entailed in their production, adds insult to grievous injury, and that, provided one's means of acquiring those items does not sustain the market for them, to consume such items – as opposed to letting them become landfill – is to show some honour or respect toward that suffering, albeit that a potential conundrum may then develop in one's claim to veganism. If veganism is defined, first and foremost, as the non-consumption of animal products, it's hard to see how one can consume-to-honour and still call oneself vegan. Should the definition of 'vegan' become more nuanced? Is it possible that, under certain circumstances, a vegan might, albeit reluctantly, 'ethically' eat meat?

Of course veganism is not a matter of the direct consumption of animal products alone. One doesn't purchase products that contain palm oil, say, because of the habitat destroyed and species threatened in its production. One doesn't purchase products employing coconuts harvested by en-slaved/abused monkeys. What is the ethical status of *these* products, if *they've* been discarded?

What of road-kill? Although the same thing could not be said of 'farm' animals who've escaped their confinement, it might be argued 'wild' or 'feral' animals killed on roads have not been raised for and suffered under the regime of human consumption, and have not been killed directly for such consumption. Does this place them in a situation similar to that of the discard? Does the 'accidental' nature of their death mean they can be eaten without moral compromise or supporting the 'conventional economy'?

It's likely, too, if one was not brought up to be vegan, but has converted in youth or adulthood, one will possess non-vegan items – a leather belt, let's say, or a pair of leather shoes. What is one to do with these? On the one hand one's decided no longer to wear or otherwise employ the products of animal suffering and it could be expected one would discard them. But on the other they *are* the products of animal suffering. It might just as validly be argued, as in the case of discarded meat, that, to honour/respect the creature whose death has enabled the production of such items, one should continue to use rather than discard them.

I won't pretend that any of these issues are simple matters. Ultimately, I suspect, and for all the Compte de Buffon's warning in this regard,[18] the resolution of such issues must lie in the character and internal dynamics of the individuals concerned – their will-power, their ability and/or predisposition to compartmentalise their ethics and actions. I would, however, offer the following.

It may be possible to maintain a determination to eat or employ or take advantage of no animal products in a manner that sustains the 'conventional' economy, yet eat or employ or take advantage of them when that economy discards them, but it's hard to see that that discarding in any way cleanses such products of the suffering the original abuse entailed or that such a recasting does not involve a quite conscious refusal to make the choice *not* to eat them, and isn't, *de facto*, a subjugation of morality to ownership and (yes) that economy itself.

The 'conventional' economy is broader than the exchange of money. It is also a matter of gesture, consistency, time. It's not inconceivable there may be people who, out of respect or honour for the suffering their production has entailed, force themselves to eat or otherwise utilise the discard-form of otherwise proscribed items, not only setting the normal form of their beliefs aside, but (secular saints?) debasing themselves, in their own eyes and the eyes of others, in order to do so. But we live in an age of surveillance, an economy of the gaze, much of it (our social media) surveillance of each other. We are *seen*, and interpreted, understood and classified accordingly. And those things – the interpretation, the understanding, the classification – are in the vast majority of cases done hastily, before any explanation can be offered. The mere fact that we may be *seen* wearing a leather belt, wearing a pair of leather shoes, or taking/eating a piece of meat, will be taken to condone their consumption – that is, interpreted according to a 'conventional economy' of human motivation and assumption – however different our real motives might be.

'Free' as discarded goods may be, it may be that the products of animal suffering should *be* left be, and that the vegan should maintain his/her/their veganness. Anything else introduces a category error, confuses the moral/ethical issue with issues of *property* and *use*, and so veers from the non-human animal at the very point we should most hold our focus.

29

A Parable of Fences

The sheep who live with me – whose agent-advocate, among humans, I find myself (what *is* my relationship to them? companion animal?) – live surrounded by fences, *to prevent them getting out* into an environment that, although they may be curious about it (sheep, I find, are very curious), would be almost certainly, and probably quite swiftly, lethal to them, and *to prevent others* (wild humans, wild dogs) *from getting in.* To 'free' them, that is to say, in as much as they can be freed, and to provide for their needs, they must be confined. That they have two acres, one cleared and one of scrubland, over which to roam – that they have a landscape, a terrain – does not much alter the fact of this confinement. On which side of the fences that surround them does freedom lie? Is freedom, in this sense, possible at all?

For farm animals, whether 'rescued' or still trapped within the Satanic mills of industry – but arguably for *all* non-human animals – the whole world is a kind of prison. That my sheep companions are in a safe zone within a vast prison doesn't alter the fact that they're within that prison. A paradox, then, that in order to free them as much as we are able we must confine them. And this is only the beginning – the larger frame – of the ethics, and ethical dilemmas, they confront us with. They grow wool. Excessively, as they're bred to. By the end of the winter they're heavy with it. It will have kept them warm when they needed it but when the heat of the summer arrives it will be oppressive to them and very likely dangerous to their health. They must therefore be shorn (I'll speak only of shearing). The better 'condition' they are in, the heavier they are; the heavier they are the harder they are to shear. To shear them they have to be man- (or woman-)handled; if they struggle against this (and who wouldn't?), even with the most careful of handling (and our shearer is very careful), they'll very likely sustain cuts from the blades, all the more so if they're merinos, who have been bred to have more skin-surface (folds) than they need, to increase the amount of wool they produce. Why must this happen? How has this situation come to be? Human use, of course: human manipulation, for economic benefit. A 'conventional economy' that sees them first and foremost as units of production. We have taken a minute number of sheep – only four! – out of that economy – brought them in to something like the space of the discard – but how can we take that economy (its shadow, its damage) out of them?

30
Intervention

Wild ducklings, and the perennial problem of intervention. The hubris in thinking that there is some superior morality in *our* perception. When the drake of one brood is systematically – instinctually? – killing the ducklings of a second, *un*draked brood, there's a countervailing instinctual *human*-animal tendency to intervene. At least, there is in me: I shouldn't speak for others. But what is to say our countervailing instinct – and the ethic driving it – is correct? Not only does it come from the same source – the ethology of the human animal – as that ethic which supports the mass slaughter of non-human animals for food, entertainment and convenience, but there's so much it doesn't know, so much it occludes in its own gut-reactions.

Could it be, for example, that the drake killing the ducklings of a drake-less brood is acting in the awareness that any refugee ducklings joining his own will stretch his and his partner's physical resources and so further threaten their own duck-lings' precarious survival? Could it be that he's conducting a kind of merciful infanticide, based on an almost-certainty that those ducklings, *without* a drake, will not survive?

Do such considerations mean one should *not* intervene? To save lives that in fact need not be lost? No. But the nature and trajectory of the intervention, like the care entailed, will be the better, surely, for any careful observation and consideration that precedes or accompanies it.

We're not – at least, not *only* – minds dealing with members of species other than our own; *we are minds dealing with minds*, the ethics motivating our actions are dealing with actions motivated by ethics that may *differ* from our own. It might help to remind ourselves that *ethics* and *ethology*, the study of the habits and culture of non-human species, bear the same etymological root, and that ethics might best be considered as species specific.

If we approach non-human animals with exclusively *human* ethics, we're likely to find ourselves, over and again, in situations in which what *we* understand as ethics will not quite do – that ethics, in this regard, are, or entail, a border to be negotiated with other species, a border we're not much used to, and still have a great deal of work to do to understand conceptually, let alone map.

Should we intervene, to save a life? Yes, I think so; but, in saying that, I'm aware of many things –

precautions and responsibilities one must take – about which I've learnt only by intervening too hastily, and making mistakes. One intervenes, most often, in a situation of some urgency (the drake is there, in the paddock, killing ducklings!), but the ramifications of the intervention may be life-long, i.e. if not as long as one's own life, then as long as those in which one intervenes.

We save the lives of two ducklings. Female. Bring them up carefully. Make mistakes, but they survive. Eventually they are adopted by a drake, who teaches them to fly and doubtless a whole lot of other things we're not able to teach them. They survive for several years. First one of these females has a brood (out of season; all of the ducklings die), then in the following year they each have broods, presumably to the same drake who adopted them.

By the time the second of these broods appears, ten days after the first, the drake, having bonded to the first, proceeds to kill the new ducklings (the scenario above). I intervene, though succeed only in scattering them and, I suspect, merely interrupt the process, though over the days that follow at least one and perhaps a second of the ducklings in the second brood is adopted into the first.

Ten days later, however, *all* of the ducklings (second *and* first brood) have died. The duck who had the brood in the previous year has, late in the summer of the second, another brood, her third. These ducklings also die. We count them as the days go by. They (for the drake is always with her) begin with eleven. On the second day they are down to nine. By the fourth there are six. Etc. It is heartbreaking to watch. Most of the deaths occur in the forest, at night, in the cold.

We know that if we intervene, try to capture and raise the ducklings ourselves, we are likely only to scatter them, lose some of them in the scrub, where they are almost impossible to find and will very likely die. Intervention might cause as much harm as it avoids. This duck, we tell ourselves, is not a good parent. She is easily distracted, flies off with the drake for an hour or more, leaving the brood exposed. To the baking sun, the cold, the wind, the dangerous (often lethal) harassment of other ducks, or to kookaburras, currawongs, butcher-birds. She doesn't even seem to know how to get the tiny ducklings underneath her, for rest and protection.

We begin at last – it takes us a while – to wonder if, in our initial intervention, when we saved and raised the two abandoned ducklings – we didn't, inadvertently, break a chain of knowledge. They survived, yes, but, brought up so much by *humans*, they had no model of *duck* maternity. How many subsequent duckling deaths did we, in this sense, *bring about* by rescuing the two we did?

There are ways out of this conundrum, as I have hinted, but they are indubitably the product of painful experience. It's not my point, here, to write of them. My point is that *any* intervention is likely to have long-term consequences of this or a similar nature.

Should one intervene? Yes, I think sometimes one should. But though most such decisions will be – and have to be – made upon gut responses, one should try to prepare oneself, or attempt to make swift contact with someone who has done so. Sometimes, hard as it is, it may be better not to.

31

The Fourth Reich

An intriguing passage in an as-yet unpublished essay:

> As the mercury was hitting thirty-seven degrees that hot afternoon, the smell of her infected and decomposing body could be sensed over forty metres away. The rescuers reached the site to find the kangaroo still breathing but unable to move. Skin and bones, badly-worn-down teeth, pouch lacerated and severely infected by maggots (as was her mouth), death for this twenty-year-old lady was imminent. Most people would likely have killed her, and by doing so have acted in compliance with the Code of Practice for Injured, Sick and Orphaned Protected Fauna, issued by the NSW Office of Environment and Heritage. The Code provides standards (mandatory action) and guidelines (advisable action) to 'achieve acceptable animal welfare levels'. In many

cases the highest level of welfare is presumably achieved by terminating the animal's life. With an emphasis on population health rather than individual health, the Code, for instance, prescribes mandatory euthanasia for animals that have lost their reproductive capacity. Animals who exhibit signs of old age and/or whose ability for long-term independent food acquisition and processing is impaired, as in the case of the kangaroo above, subsequently named Thelma, should also be euthanized.[19]

An 'emphasis on population health rather than individual health', 'mandatory euthanasia for animals that have lost their reproductive capacity', animals 'who exhibit signs of old age', 'whose ability for long-term independent food acquisition and processing is impaired'. The elderly. The disabled. The sick. Although it would appear that the Code of Practice from the New South Wales Office of Environment and Heritage as represented above is neither mandatory nor inflexible, and that its guidelines can be set aside in certain circumstances, its recommendations bear more than a little resemblance to certain of the policies of National Socialism. We execrated such policies when we found out about them, and continue to, when applied to humans, but it seems we're prepared to adopt them for other animals. A disjunct. An ethical taboo on the human side, freed up again when it crosses the species barrier.

But hasn't this always been the way? Eugenics, which we abhorred in the Third Reich, has been a central part of animal husbandry as long as we've had the concept. The selection – breeding up – of certain traits, the elimination of others. What we see as utterly unacceptable when practiced upon humans has long been regarded as a norm when it comes to animals.[20]

Is it too far-fetched to call this realm, this place-of-the-animals, the Fourth Reich? I must admit I'm not entirely comfortable with the term myself. On the one hand – coming after the Third, a Fifth potentially following – it suggests a sequence, historicity, an ultimate limitation, or at least the possibility of *interruption*, of times *between*, whereas this place-of-the-animals, to borrow Isaac Bashevis Singer's term, is (or has seemed) eternal, and on the other hand there's a kind of unstated rule, out in 'normal' human society, that you can't compare animal suffering to human suffering, and to the Shoah in particular, although ironically, and as I've said above, it was survivors of the Shoah who first made this link. But the comparison nevertheless keeps coming back to me. If it seems to over-state then it may be that it is the recipient, not the maker of the statement, who must make the adjustment. The hell of so many animals cannot be overstated. We speak of a fourth dimension to things; isn't the place-of-the-animals a kind of dark fourth dimension to our humanness? A dark realm (*reich*) with humans the oppressors, the self-appointed master race?

32
Suspension

At the bottom of a long stretch of boredom (but is it truly boredom, if motivated by curiosity, desire to know?), self-imposed, watching sheep, forcing oneself to do so, to stay there, in the middle of the paddock, below the water-tank, resisting the pressure to *get on with* one's active, understood, human-animal life – it's a kind of meditation, yes, although even to think of it thus is to distract – there's the possibility of seeing, noticing something that one has not noticed before: Henry's sudden limping (could that be a pulled muscle? a stitch?) or the rhythm of their grazing, two snips upward and one back, like a barber (is it the same for them all or do they have different *techniques*?) and their rumination, their chewing, two of them clockwise, the others anti-clockwise (are there left-handed sheep and right-handed sheep? Jason who was anti-clockwise yesterday is clockwise today); and the *moods* Orpheus wakes in, carries through the day, do they come from something he's dreamt about, or might he have headaches, a tooth-ache? and Jonathan, is it really true that, when you stroke his ears, his cheek, he has begun to purr, like a cat? Henry's nose runs all winter, on the colder days (as does mine)…

Sheep thoughts. There are duck thoughts, too, and magpie thoughts, dog thoughts. Would that there could be kangaroo thoughts as well, but I 'know' them in a different way, mediated, laden with the static of human interest: I am *surprised* at all I have come to 'know', 'about' them, but it's all provisional, hearsay, from reliable sources it may be, but hearsay. Still, possible. Knowing prepares us to know.

33
Equality

When I say – if I *do* say – that non-human animals are our equals, what do I mean by this? What, for example, *is* my relationship with the non-human animals with whom I find myself living? *In what sense* do I live with them? In what sense do I *not* live with them? I try to avoid terms and constructions of this relationship – terms and constructions such as 'protector', 'guardian' – which carry their own power relation, and although the mind, and the voice which gives it expression, too often slip into the easy shorthand (/persiflage) of '*my* sheep', '*our* sheep', they (the mind, the voice) are left, as often as not, to deal with the feeling that they have just (yet again...) betrayed the non-humans they've been referring to.

It is not, I think, that one *can* avoid the relationship's being, from any way you look at it, one of substantial and one-sided power, though I'd hope it's possible to shift the way one conceives it more toward obligation: that is, that one has advantages, abilities, given the parameters within which we are all forced to live, which one (the human animal) is obliged to bring, where possible, to the assistance of the non-human animal.

A very important question we might all ask ourselves is *Do we really feel that non-human animals are our equals?* And while an honest answer would have to be, almost universally, No, we might progress to asking ourselves *why* we don't feel them to be so, and what *we* might do to change this situation.

34

Humanness

One of the greatest risks to refuge is our own humanness – the way refuge itself can become hostage to the vicissitudes of our own lives, our relationships, our health, our finances, our convenience. A promising sanctuary closes when one of the two founders – life partners – develops cancer. Another collapses when the marriage upon which it's financially and in other ways dependent breaks down. Another closes when a dispute arises between its founders. Another as a means of *saving* a marriage. Another when the person who has run it for decades becomes too frail to continue. Humans are like that. *Life* is like that. Someone *will* fall in love. Someone *will* have an affair. Someone *will* have an accident, or a stroke, or develop cancer. Someone *will* be offered a job they can't refuse. People *will* argue over finances, workloads, levels of commitment. And in most cases the non-humans in their care must be relocated, creating further pressure on other sanctuaries as often as not already stretched to their limit. Creatures who were offered safety, care and calm for the rest of their lives must be moved again, *their* friendships and relationships and life-threads disrupted once more; trust that's been so carefully established is broken once more, hopes that had begun to return are dashed once more.

The lives of non-human animals are not secondary. To run a refuge is a deep commitment. If it takes a particular kind of person to set up and sustain such a place – resilient, independent, seemingly inexhaustible, profoundly dedicated to non-human animals, superhumanly selfless – it also takes a particular set of relationships about them, perhaps even to the point of avoidance of relationships. But even these people are human. And very careful thought, in establishing and maintaining a refuge, must be given to avoiding or offsetting the dangers of this humanness.

Some very careful *structural* consideration, for example. Someone may *found* a sanctuary – perform that immense and visionary task – but there's an argument for establishing a board or management committee, so the place is not at the mercy of that one person's fate, although a board or management committee means involvement of other people and it's also a sad fact of humanness that the greater the number of people involved, the more likely disputes, jealousies, power-plays (etc.) will arise.

Do 'animal' people need to be particularly cautious in this regard? Paradoxical and counter-intuitive as it may seem, disputes of such kinds appear to be so prevalent, where non-human animals are concerned, that one wonders if there isn't something deep in the cultural substrate – bulwarked as it is against non-human animals – that, like a circuit-breaker in a fuse-box, trips up their human advocates.

Perhaps the best one can do is to be aware of this propensity and seek actively to prepare oneself against it – to be aware above all that this propensity is in all likelihood far more institutional and situational, and far less personal, than may initially appear.

There has been some interesting theorising in this regard. Bill Moyer, author of the *Movement Action Plan* (1986), suggests that there are four roles essential to the development and success of any social movement – *Reformer* (advocate), *Citizen* (helper), *Change Agent* (organiser), and *Rebel* – and that these roles have varying importance at different stages in that movement's progress. Much of the conflict within such movements, he argues – and this might be extrapolated to many a group of animal rights workers/advocates – occurs between one role and another and can be eased by a better understanding of these roles and the factors that bring about changes in the relationships between them.[21]

It might also be, in 'animal' movements, that such dissonances are in some part the flip-side of the intensity of care involved, and a by-product of the beleagueredness abovementioned. 'Animal' people feel passionately about the work they do. They also encounter little encouragement, indeed great resistance, from the societies in which they operate. The very strength with which their passion is resisted can cause it to be internalised, not only by the individuals concerned but also by the wider groups in which they operate.

'Animal' people work with a felt urgency – they are dealing with lives, after all, and often also with situations that require that they place themselves at risk, both physically and legally. They need to be aware of the psychological stress this creates and the necessity of developing ways to manage this stress. Non-human animals need all the help they can get, and much the same goes for those who provide that help. In the midst of such urgency these carers are not necessarily the best judges of the help they receive, and in truth have scant right to reject or discourage it. If we find the work thankless (for example), we might ask ourselves why we need that thanks, and set that aside. It has to be enough – *is* more than enough – to see fellow beings we've had the privilege of helping survive into another day, another month, injuries heal, shredded psyches become more calm and more integrated – or die, if and when that is or has to be the case, an easier, more dignified, less painful death than they might have had without us. Out here – there – in the Open we're not alone but part of a tribe more vast than, from our human cage, we could ever have imagined.

35
Trolley Problems

Although the basic idea is so simple it could be centuries old,[22] the best-known modern form of what's come to be called the Trolley Problem was presented by Philippa Foot in 1967.[23] In this version we're asked to imagine standing at a switch beside a railway track. A trolley (a tram, a train) is heading directly down the track toward a group of five people who are oblivious to its approach. If we pull the switch the trolley will be diverted to a siding upon which there is only one person standing, likewise unaware of the trolley's approach. We're asked to choose between doing nothing, in which case five people will die, or diverting the trolley, in which case only one will die. Apparently over ninety percent of respondents say they'd divert the trolley, kill one to save five.

In one of the many variants of this problem[24] we're not beside the track but on a footbridge above it. There's no switch there. Diverting the trolley isn't an option. We could throw ourselves onto the track to try to stop the trolley before it hits the group of five, but we're too light and it's clear this won't work. There is, on the other hand, a large, heavy man standing beside us. If we grab this man and throw him onto the track, the trolley will be stopped. The heavy man will be killed but five people will be saved. Do we do this? In effect murder one person to save the lives of five others?

There's a step, however, that none of the discussions of the problem I've so far encountered have taken, an *animal* step, that would seem, *if* taken, to exemplify, yet again, the manner in which serious consideration of non-human animals can throw a spanner into our ethical works.

This isn't to say some thinkers haven't already in some manner introduced animals into the equation. One, for example – with a few too many problems to take aboard here (the continued suffering and instrumentalisation, ready supply and easy replacement of the mice, etc.) – has put laboratory mice on one track, humans on the other, and wondered what weight should be given to the possibility that, saved, a laboratory mouse might, by virtue of the experiments performed upon him/her, 'save' many humans. Another replaces the five humans with five higher-order primates. Another replaces them with a critically-endangered species. Still another replaces them with one's beloved pet.

All very well, but from an 'animalist' perspective a vital and rather obvious option is missing.

Let's assume that, like the great majority of the population of most Western countries (most countries, period), the five people on the track are carnists – eaters of the flesh and/or consumers of the products of non-human animals (it need not be all five: the point will hold if only one is carnist). And let's assume that these carnists are in, say, their twenties (or thirties, or forties), which is to say that, if their lives are saved, it could be expected those lives would continue for another twenty, thirty or forty years.

During each one of those years, each of these people saved will consume a certain number of non-human animals (fish, prawns and other sea creatures, chickens, portions of sheep, cattle, pigs, etc.). Over a lifetime – to put this very conservatively – the number of non-human creatures consumed by a carnist might extend to several thousand.

It's reasonable to assume that in saving the lives of five *carnists* one is in effect condemning to death many animals: hundreds, if the continuing lives of those five people turn out to be very short ones, thousands – perhaps *many* thousands – if their lives continue for a decade or so.

The possibility exists, all this is to say, that someone thinking more broadly might come to the conclusion that many more lives will be saved by allowing the trolley to plough *into* the group of five people than by diverting it so that it kills only the one.

Do we object to this? Upon what grounds? 'Human exceptionalism'? That to present the trolley problem in this way is a kind of category error? That we humans are more important than non-human animals? That we should save our own species first and foremost, regardless of the consequences for other species?

The human bubble. If we criticise human exceptionalism, as a great many animal activists and advocates do, while at the same time excepting humans, how are our declarations of rights and equality for non-human animals anything more than promises made with our fingers crossed behind our backs?

Is this a situation we can do something about? Probably not. It's a floodgate, after all, and to open it is to alter our situation entirely. But, *if* not, how can we, while at the same time pursuing our goals of approach and redress to non-human animals, adjust the terms of our promises to reflect and guard against the taint, and mitigate the continuing damage, of this embarrassing hypocrisy?

Another situation we need to face, and (again) keep thinking...

36
Writing Animals

There occur, in our sentences, as we write non-human animals, stubbornnesses, like rocks in our path, that are also stubbornnesses in our minds, our thinking. Small, they might seem at first, but in fact they are on the edges of, and testament that we are entering, something vast. We're at the edge of, on the verge of (will we take it on or not?), one of the greatest changes in human direction, to turn toward – turn *back* to? (back? was there ever?) – the animal/ animals, a pivotal moment because it has been our turning away from them (and a turning that turning-away into use, consumption) that's at once enabled us to get as far as we have and has doomed that going. That this (re)turn begins with, is based upon, is intricately connected to, *diet* is an amazing thing, an astonishing simplicity, but, for the here and now of *this* writing, neither here nor there. (Yesterday, the gaze from the boys – the sheep – as I went out onto the veranda to make a call. The tension, the felt choice, there: whether to respond *with* the gaze, or to go down, greet them, a choice in essence – so it seemed in that moment – between thought [therefore maintaining separation, distance, objectification] and love, encounter, never so unam-biguously acknowledged as when the eyes *close*.)

In writing, are we (/can we be) *approaching* – i.e. writing against itself – or are we simply maintaining the distance? Writing must interrogate itself, *in the animals' gaze* (or absence thereof), find a way of so doing without becoming a coat, a veneer that seals a barrier between. It must proceed as if it were something that does not know itself, must reduce itself to a crawl, can learn only by going.

37
Rituals of Repression

Auschwitz begins when someone looks at a slaughterhouse and says 'They're only animals.'
– Theodor Adorno[25]

How *is* it we can look at slaughterhouses? How is it we can even tolerate their existence? And yet of course – and although in large part it's a *tacit* toleration and the look is rather a *disinclination* that, the closer to the slaughterhouse we find ourselves, becomes more and more like refusal – we do. A great many of us – sometimes it seems the vast majority – enjoy, even celebrate, their product and the products of what we might call their affiliated institutions (the dairy, the egg farm), consuming, often two or three times in a twenty-four-hour period, the flesh of non-human animals or the products of their labour and their pain.

By and large, in all truth, we are not totally unaware of where these products come from and the suffering they entail. By and large, too, we do not see ourselves as cruel people, and do not consciously will this suffering upon the creatures we utilise in this way.

How is it we are able to reconcile these two apparently conflicting aspects of our being? Would it surprise us (an hypothesis) to find that, almost as ubiquitously, we build into our days what, if we were aware of them, we might think of as *rituals of repression* of those parts of the mind and conscience which, balking at such slaughter and abuse, might make our very eating intolerable to us?

Consider just one possibility.

Where once, not many decades ago, a robbery, a kidnapping, an act of arson (etc.) might have been seen as a sufficient crime upon which to base an evening television detective story, one could be forgiven for thinking that now – as if something has begun to shift in our deep subconscious – nothing but murder will do. Night after night, supported by an apparently limitless corroboration from the 'reality' of our newspapers and news sites, we are fed a rich, and deeply ritualised, diet of death.

In program after program, film after film, we witness a person or persons *turned into body, made carcase*, by parties as yet unknown, the discovery and identification of the victim and determination that a crime has been committed followed by the meticulous analysis and 'solving' of that crime and the identification, apprehension and social seques-tration (punishment) of the criminal(s). A ritual, *comedic* in the classical sense. The social fabric, torn by a murderous deed (someone *turned into corpse, into meat-like thing*), is – by police, by detectives, forensic pathologists, lawyers, judges – carefully and methodically restitched.

Although we're reluctant to look directly upon the immense suffering our appetite wreaks upon non-human animals, it seems we're prepared, indeed demand, night after night, the opportunity to view and symbolically process its simulacrum, containing and expiating what we do, clearing the psychic decks, much as the killing floor is cleaned, for the next day's work.

I'll readily admit that some of the deeper functions of this nightly engorgement[26] aren't clear. Are we, by seeing such things enacted over and again, *inuring* ourselves to the horror our appetites demand? Are we *reinforcing* our sense of a violation of 'reason' and 'order' in treating, in the act of murder, the *human as if it were animal*? Are we confirming, through the re-stitching of the social fabric, that humans are *not* animals, that only *animals* are slaughtered (*and/but* that animals *are* slaughtered)? Are we *confessing* at one level what, at another, we have been hiding from ourselves (the animal dimension of the human, the barbarity and repulsiveness of what we do to non-human animals)? Very likely it's several of these things at once.

38

Sorrow

Do you think the sheep are happy? T. asks me, and
the answer, as I'm seeing it, has to be *No, for some
of the time – much of the time? – I think they're not.*
Not that I'd always have answered so. It's been a
gradual, even reluctant realisation. That the other
side of the fact and process of sanctuary, the happiness and release of it, is the way it exposes, allows
to come into focus, the misery that has hitherto
been visited upon so many of the individuals, and
species, who've found their way to it. In a place of
sanctuary they can discover – grow into, recover, be
– what they are, yet so much of what they are is
sorrow, the legacy of abuse.

Give the abused sanctuary and, yes, some recovery is possible; but the *im*possible (of recovery, of
escape, of redress) also becomes apparent. Sanctuary
may be the place where animals can escape further
damage, but it's also – since it's a place of attention,
observation – a place where the suffering is *seen*.[27]
We would give our sheep anything and everything

we can but there are so many things that cannot be returned to them. It goes without question that those who attempt to care for these non-human companions also expose themselves to this misery and its non-escapable portion, the angst and frustration of being only able to help so far. But that is a human matter. Let's hope *that* pain is the pain of transition.

39
Reversal

So hard to learn, some of these lessons, and yet so simple. Today's (this week's, this month's) that, over and again, one should stop, turn back, quell one's first, *conditioned* impulse and prioritise some thing which, normally, one would have abandoned, overlooked, in order to follow that other. Don't, when a thought comes, close the door on the boys (the sheep who live with us) and go back to the desk to write it down (prioritising the thought), but continue sitting with them, murmuring to them, stroking their ear or cheek, or simply being, still or otherwise, not touching, until *they* are ready to wander off; *don't* go up to get that telephone, make or answer that call, instead turn back to put something – a thought like this, *here*, small as it is, reversing a reversal – down. Put (lest that last seem a contradiction) *first* the thing you were about to put *second* (or not do at all), *second* the thing you were about to put *first*. Amplify the quiet, turn down the louder, so you can hear. We are taught to relegate the non-human animal, and the animal self, but how can we *approach* when so much distracts us? How much can we hear when it's *we* who choose the moment (and place, and mode) of the conversation?

40
Painism

Do I focus too much upon slaughter, upon the pain and suffering of non-human animals? I find it hard to see how there *can* be 'too much' focus upon it, that it is a central issue of our being, but perhaps this concentration of focus creates problems of its own.

Richard Ryder, thirty years ago, coined the term *painism* in arguing for rights of non-human animals based upon his conviction that all animals who can feel pain should be protected from the imposition *of* pain. In the early 1990s, in Oxford, he feels it's important to have such a position as a kind of third way, a challenge, as he puts it, to 'both utilitarianism[28] [like that of Peter Singer] and democracy by insisting that pains, pleasures and happiness cannot meaningfully be totalled across individuals. So there is no justification for causing pain to one individual for the mere convenience of many.'[29]

Fair enough, as far as it goes, but I've found the term, in my own thinking, has spread, almost against itself, to encompass a tendency, in the minds and work of advocates, activists and others concerned with the rights and the suffering of non-human creatures, to focus upon the pain and suffering of those creatures, almost to the exclusion of all else.

That the pain and suffering of non-human animals, especially those trapped within the processes of industrial farming, must be foregrounded there is no question. But – such is the mess-of-thought our so-largely-unthinking cruelty has created, for us *and* them – that very centrality and overridingness creates problems of its own, must be so carefully handled, even as it's acted upon, because central to its impact is a victimhood, a deprivation or discounting of the very agency which is, arguably, pivotal in establishing that essential, recognisable, core *being* that we seem to need non-human animals to be able to demonstrate in order to guarantee the rights and 'equality' we claim for them.

The problem here – an inherent paradox? – is not unique to painism, but could be seen as a broader issue concerning the institutionalisation of animal rights per se. At a time when we're most concerned to *dismantle* the species barrier, the formalisation of rights of non-human animals, well-intentioned as it is, can be seen as the erection *of* a barrier. Such rights protect *them* from *us*. This may be a legal barrier only, but its effects are in-determinate. Arguably, in formalising those rights, we're formalising the position of non-human animals as victim, *setting into law their want of agency*, continuing to define them, as we always have, as *lack*. Am I arguing against the establishment of animal rights? Hardly! But it's a tricky business.

Can we avoid painism? I'm not sure we can. But we can do our best to maintain a kind of double focus, keep in mind both the suffering animals and those others, the non-victim portions of them, *who are not there*, or, if that is too much to say, the fullness of whose subjecthood has been obscured by that victimisation. As we focus, as we have to, upon the pain and the suffering – as we do all we can to *make others see* – we must also try to stay aware, not only of the inherent contradictions and paradoxes involved, but of the shadow animal that this pain and suffering effaces, the non-victim that domestication has denied, the being that the industrial process suffocates and the slaughter cuts short, the adulthood that this perpetual massacre of innocents renders impossible, the tribal culture it obliterates, the emotional and psychic life it shreds almost before it can begin.

41

Collaboration

An ant, seen crossing a wide, clear stretch of soil between patches of grass, carrying with two of her six legs – the front two, her arms if you ask me – a fragment of a dried leaf twice as high and almost as long as she is, stopping now and again to shift the load, get a better grip, or rest and then pick it up again, coming eventually to a stick as high as ant and leaf-fragment together, and such a long way to get around that, assessing the situation, she decides she has no option but to go up and over. She starts pushing the load before her but it's too heavy and unwieldy. Another ant appears out of somewhere – she's come out of her way – and gives her a hand. Together they manage to get the unwieldy fragment up to the top of the stick and to slide it to the ground on the other side. The pair then go their separate ways, the first carrying the leaf-fragment as before, the second back over the stick and off toward one of the patches of grass.

And there are those who will tell you that *mind*, that *consciousness* are not involved.

42
The Horse

'What matters', I wrote at the beginning of this work, 'is what Nietzsche said to the horse.' Perhaps the wrong approach entirely. What if what truly matters is what the *horse* said to *Nietzsche*? Or rather, since that would have been nothing, given that horses can't speak in any language human animals can readily understand, *what that nothing said*, what it *exposed*, to drive Nietzsche mad, or send him so darkly sane: to take away *his* power of speech?

I like to think of it, this Nietzschean moment – this Nothing – as a sudden encounter, at once epiphanic and utterly disgrounding, with, on the one hand, the force and intensity of another animal's *being*, and on the other a yawning gap, a terrible, concomitant blindness, a profound *guilt-in-oneself*, as if some substrate of one's own being (an assumption of its rightness and centrality) has collapsed or been abruptly removed, the apprehension of the other's being entailing, as it does, realization of our complicity in the (ab)use of and mindless cruelty toward that other, and the way this in its turn has meant the abandonment of some key thing in our *own* being – an existential *validity* – without which we are, and have, nothing.

This encounter, the gaze toward animals, will be a double encounter. It will seem – *be* – so much an encounter with nothing, but that nothing is an affect of the perceiver, not the perceived. Seeming to *give* us nothing, *produce* nothing (they will not *answer*), to be fruit*less*, its fruit, paradoxically, will be that Nothing which we have built our civilization as a wall against: that Nothing which now has to be the thing that teaches us, that dark, fig-like fruit which, opened, contains so many *seeds*.

NOTES

1 Translated by R. J. Hollingdale, from *A Nietzsche Reader*, ed. Hollingdale (Penguin, 1977), 55.

2 Melanie Joy (*Why We Love Dogs, Eat Pigs, and Wear Cows*, Conari, 2009) uses this term to indicate that the decision to eat meat is a matter of belief and choice – one *believes* one needs to eat it, and *chooses* to do so – rather than something (a 'biological necessity') inherent/essential to the species.

3 The English title of Blanchot's essay had so powerful a ring that it lodged in the theoretical culture almost immediately, as if it captured a profound truth. But this title was a translation. The French title is '*Le regard d'Orphée*', and *regard* may be variously translated as *look*, *glance*, or *gaze*, even *regard* itself. Could some of the power of the title and the concept have come, not so much from an essence in the essay itself, as from the translator's choice?

4 The essay 'Repressive Tolerance' was Marcuse's contribution to *A Critique of Pure Tolerance*, by Robert Paul Wolff, Barrington Moore Jr, and Herbert Marcuse (Beacon Press, 1965).

5 Indebted, for some references, to http://www.singingtothe plants.com/2012/06/thinking-about-death-i-heidegger/

6 *Being and Time* (1927) II.i (47), 240-1, trans. Stambaugh (SUNY, 1996) 224. See also *Being and Time* II.i (48/9), 246-7 (Stambaugh 228-9).

7 Perhaps another of the reasons that Philosophy insists upon the separation of the work from the *person*, i.e. that once something has entered the articulated (/controlled) realm of the work it has escaped the crisis – the critical moment – of that *saying*.

8 Banned from 1945 until 1951 from university teaching, Heidegger gave these lectures privately, to a select audience.

9 Neske, G., & E. Kettering, eds, *Martin Heidegger and National Socialism: Questions and answers* (Paragon House, 1990), xxix; A. Milchman & A. Rosenberg, 'Heidegger, Planetary Technics, and the Holocaust', in A. Milchman and A. Rosenberg, eds, *Martin Heidegger and the Holocaust* (Humanities Press International, 1996), 218; G. Leaman, 'Strategies of deception: The composition of Heidegger's silence', in Milchman & Rosenberg, 60.

10 Neske & Kettering, xxx; Leaman, 59; Milchman & Rosenberg, 217.

11 Sonnet II.13, in Stephen Mitchell's translation: *Duino Elegies & Sonnets to Orpheus* (New York: Vintage International, 2009).

12 Stambaugh 229.

13 *Twilight of the Idols* (1889), trans. R.J. Hollingdale (Penguin, 1968), 63.

14 Trans (as *Daybreak*) R.J. Hollingdale (Cambridge University Press, 1982), 5.

15 The reader can perhaps intuit the meaning of this term. See my essay 'The Fallacies: theory, saturation capitalism and non-human animals', in *Animal Dreams* (Sydney University Press, 2021).

16 Reflections perhaps more commonly occurring in a variation, i.e. that the piece of meat/cheese such people find in front of and tempting them 'will go to waste' in any case, the animal having already died/been exploited, and so it may as well be they who consume it.

17 But difference to what? We are compound – many, many, many faceted. *Which* 'us', or facets of us, does this othering refer to? *All* of them? Arguably the notion that non-human animals are in some way our Other is so broad and so general as to have

little real meaning other than as an intellectual plaything: a balloon, inflated, essentially empty.

18 '*Le style c'est l'homme même*': 'the style *is* the man' (or woman, or...), which is to say that if one divides one's actions, compartmentalises one's ethics, it may be that one divides and compartmentalises oneself.

19 'Not by Milk Alone: Attachment Relations and Wildlife Rehabilitation', by T. Brooks-Pribac, H. Bergen and R. Mjadwesch.

20 A point as pertinent to Australia's (and New Zealand's) privileging of native over exotic species in their conservation policy, to the extent of eradication/elimination of exotic (non-native) species in the attempt to return their ecosystems to pre-settlement states, a policy which, in the *human* realm, could be condemned as ethnic cleansing.

21 See Moyer (ed.), *Doing democracy: the MAP model for organizing social movements* (New Society Publishers, 2001).

22 In one account it originated as a teaching device at the University of Wisconsin in 1905.

23 'The Problem of Abortion and the Doctrine of the Double Effect', *Oxford Review* 5 (1967).

24 Judith Jarvis Thomson, 'Killing, Letting Die, and the Trolley Problem', *The Monist* 59.2 (1976).

25 Disputed. It's claimed that this quotation was contrived for PETA's 'Holocaust on your Plate' campaign (2003) and falsely attributed to Adorno. In the 68th of Adorno's *Minima Moralia* (1951), however, one does find the following:

> The possibility of pogroms is decided in the moment when the gaze of a fatally-wounded animal falls on a human being. The defiance with which he repels this gaze – 'After all, it's only an animal' – reappears irresistibly in cruelties done to human beings.

139

26 *Murder She Wrote*, *The Midsomer Murders*, *Death in Paradise*, *Poirot*, *Miss Marple*, *NCIS*, *Law & Order*, *Hawaii Five-O*: the titles are legion and hardly confined to any one language, country or culture.

27 'It may be easier to understand the extent of the violence and deprivation animals face within the industry when you look at these same animals in a sanctuary setting after they've been rescued. The damage becomes much more obvious when they are at last allowed autonomy; when they are given the freedom, for example, to not be touched by a human', Patty Mark, 'Dreams and Beyond', *Southerly*, 74.3 (2014), 106-107.

28 Utilitarianism. That one's moral choices should be determined by what will bring the greatest happiness to the greatest number, a mode of ethical thought – thinking *about* ethics – associated primarily with Jeremy Bentham who also (coincidentally?) made one of the key assertions concerning our consideration of non-human animals, stating famously, in his *Introduction to the Principles of Morals and Legislation* (1787), 'The question is not, Can they reason?, nor Can they talk? but, Can they suffer?'

29 'Summary', *Speciesism, Painism and Happiness* (Imprint Academic, 2011), ix.

INDEX

ABOUT THE AUTHOR

David Brooks is a poet, novelist, short-fiction writer and essayist. He has taught literature at various Australian universities, and from 1999 until 2018 was co-editor of *Southerly*, the premier journal of Australian literature and new Australian writing. His work has been widely anthologised and translated, and won or been shortlisted for numerous awards. In 2014 he was awarded an Australia Council Fellowship for his distinguished contribution to Australian and international literature. Currently Honorary Associate Professor in Australian Literature at the University of Sydney, he is a vegan and animal rights advocate, and he lives in the Blue Mountains of New South Wales.

www.ingramcontent.com/pod-product-compliance
Lightning Source LLC
Chambersburg PA
CBHW060044030426
42334CB00019B/2477